SpringerBriefs in Economics

Development Bank of Japan Research Series

This series is characterized by the close academic cohesion of financial economics, environmental economics, and accounting, which are the three major fields of research of the Research Institute of Capital Formation (RICF) at the Development Bank of Japan (DBJ). Readers can acquaint themselves with how a financial intermediary efficiently restructuring firms in financial distress, can contribute to economic development.

The aforementioned three research fields are closely connected with one another in the following ways. DBJ has already developed several corporation-rating methods, including the environmental rating by which DBJ decides whether or not to make concessions to the candidate firm. To evaluate the relevance of this rating, research, which deploys not only financial economics but also environmental economics, is necessary.

The accounting section intensively studies the structure of IFRS and Integrated Reporting to predict their effects on Japanese corporate governance. Although the discipline of accounting is usually isolated from financial economics, structural and reliable prediction is never achieved without sufficient and integrated knowledge in both fields.

Finally, the environmental economics section is linked to the accounting section in the following manner. To establish green accounting (environmental accounting), it is indispensable to explore what the crucial factors for the preservation of environment (e.g. emission control) are. RICF is well-equipped to address the acute necessity for discourse among researchers who belong to these three different fields.

More information about this series at http://www.springer.com/series/13542

Masaoki Tamura

Economic Signals

Prize Promotions, Anonymous Giving, and Political Advertisements

DBJ

Springer

Masaoki Tamura
Nagoya University of Commerce and Business
Nisshin, Aichi
Japan

and

Research Institute of Capital Formation
Development Bank of Japan
Tokyo
Japan

ISSN 2191-5504 ISSN 2191-5512 (electronic)
SpringerBriefs in Economics
ISSN 2367-0967 ISSN 2367-0975 (electronic)
Development Bank of Japan Research Series
ISBN 978-981-10-8937-4 ISBN 978-981-10-8938-1 (eBook)
https://doi.org/10.1007/978-981-10-8938-1

Library of Congress Control Number: 2018935957

Printed on acid-free paper

This Springer imprint is published by the registered company Springer Nature Singapore Pte Ltd.
part of Springer Nature
The registered company address is: 152 Beach Road, #21-01/04 Gateway East, Singapore 189721, Singapore

Preface

This book sheds light on the new aspects of the three specific economic behaviors: firms' prize promotions, anonymous giving, and political advertisements. They are respectively considered as signals that firms send to consumers, donators send to others, and politicians send to voters. I show why firms, donators, and politicians create signals through these behaviors, and evaluate the economic roles and social consequences of these economic behaviors from the viewpoint of economic theory. The problems and economic environments that form the basis of these topics are firms' time inconsistency under monopoly, asymmetric information on individual altruism, and asymmetric information of politicians' types. Each topic can be seen as an application of simple economic theory to unusual subject matters in economics.

The methods used in this book include time inconsistency and signaling. The concept of time inconsistency is developed by Kydland and Prescott (1977). They point out that using the optimal control theory is problematic because economic agents foresee the future to some extent. Agents' behavior is determined by not only the past variables but also future expectations. In this book, time inconsistency is applied to the relationship between the firm and its consumers. On the other hand, the concept of signaling is developed by Spence (1973, 1974). Under asymmetric information, economic agents pay the cost to reveal their hidden type to others. Education can be regarded as one type of signaling. Even if education does not directly improve the productivity of people, educational backgrounds can be a signal for the people and informative to employers. In this book, signaling is applied to the relationship between donors and others as well as politicians and voters.

I am deeply grateful to Prof. Masayuki Otaki. Many of the ideas contained in this book stem from my dissertation at the University of Tokyo. Professor Masayuki Otaki was my supervisor, and he gave me much insightful and constructive advice. I also thank him for his suggestion to me to write this book. I am intellectually indebted for this book to Prof. Susumu Cato, Prof. Shinichi Fukuda, Prof. Kazuya Kamiya, Prof. Toshihiro Matsumura, Prof. Daisuke Miyakawa, and seminar participants at the Research Institute of Capital Formation, the Development Bank of

Japan, and Hitotsubashi University. Finally, I would like to thank the organizers at the Research Institute of Capital Formation, the Development Bank of Japan, as well as editors for their help and patience in writing this book.

Nisshin, Japan Masaoki Tamura

References

Kydland, F., & Prescott, E. C. (1977). Rules rather than discretion: The inconsistency of optimal plans. *The Journal of Political Economy, 85*(3), 473–492.

Spence, M. (1973). Job market signaling. *The Quarterly Journal of Economics, 87*(3), 355–374.

Spence, M. (1974) *Market signalling*. Cambridge: Harvard University Press.

Contents

About the Author

Masaoki Tamura is an Assistant Professor at Nagoya University of Commerce and Business and Visiting Scholar of the Research Institute of Capital Formation, the Development Bank of Japan. Born in 1982, he received a Bachelor's degree in economics at Kyoto University in 2005, Master's degrees in economics at the University of Tokyo in 2007 and at London School of Economics and Political Science in 2009 and a Ph.D. in economics at the University of Tokyo in 2014. He worked for Hitotsubashi University and Kyoto University before joining Nagoya University of Commerce and Business.

Chapter 1
Tools Used in This Book

Abstract This chapter introduces the two theoretical methods used in this book. The first method is time inconsistency in a dynamic environment that is developed by Kydland and Prescott (1977). Time inconsistency occurs when, in a dynamic environment, policy makers have incentives to deviate from their initial announcements. Here, the announcements are not credible to the agents, and called "inconsistent". An example is the government flood control and people's house building. The second method is signaling under incomplete information that is developed by Spence (1973, 1974). A sender has private information that is unobservable to others. He/she sends a message (signal) to a receiver. An example of private information and signals is workers' productivity and their education. I overview these methods and prepare for Chaps. 2, 3, and 4, where these methods are applied to prize promotions, anonymous giving, and political advertisements.

Keywords Time inconsistency · Signaling · Incomplete information game

1.1 Time Inconsistency

Optimal control theory is a simple and strong method in economic analysis. For example, by setting the lifetime utility function and lifetime budget constraint, economists model the situation in which consumers decide their lifetime consumption plan at the begging of the life stage. This type of modeling is applied in many studies in economics. However, Kydland and Prescott (1977) point out that the important assumption of the optimal control theory is that the current decision depends only on the current and past decisions and situations. However, in many economic situations, this environment is not satisfied. For example, consumers and firms care about future economic situations and economic policies including the tax and fiscal policies. In such situations, the optimal control theory is inappropriate.

Time inconsistency occurs when, in a dynamic environment, policy makers deviate from the initial expectations of agents. Suppose there are two periods, current and future, and two agents, consumers and the government. In each period, both consumers and the government make decisions. The government (sometimes implicitly)

M. Tamura, *Economic Signals*, Development Bank of Japan Research Series, https://doi.org/10.1007/978-981-10-8938-1_1

announces the current and future policies. When consumers make current decisions, they observe this current policy and, at the same time, forecast the future policy. However, in the end, it is possible that policy makers deviate from agents' past expectations. In this case, the initial government announcement is "inconsistent" because in a rational expectations environment, it is not an equilibrium because agents expectations do not come true. The "consistent" policy is one that is initially announced by the government, rationally forecasted by agents, and actually carried out by the government in the end.

I present a general model of time inconsistency in the same manner as Kydland and Prescott (1977). There are two periods (t = 1, 2) in which the policy maker and agent make decisions sequentially in each period. The policy maker decides policies p_1 and p_2 for each period, and the agent decides on x_1 and x_2. Note that in many economic situations, the agent's objective function, and thus the agent's decision depends not only on the past decision and policy but also on the expectation of future policy. Therefore, the agent's decision is written as

$$x_1 = x_1(p_1, p_2), \tag{1.1}$$

$$x_2 = x_2(x_1, p_1, p_2), \tag{1.2}$$

where x_1 depends on not only the current policy but also the expectation of future policy p_2. Here, I assume that the policy maker's objective function takes the following form:

$$S(x_1, x_2, p_1, p_2). \tag{1.3}$$

Then, I consider the "optimal" policy (in this book, it is referred to as the "first best" policy). The **first best policy** is the hypothetical policy plan in which I assume that the policy maker can make credible promises p_1 and p_2 at the beginning of time period $t = 1$. It does not deviate from the initial plan at $t = 2$ and can be considered as a policy commitment. The first order condition (FOC) with respect to p_2, one of the policy variables, is

$$\frac{\partial S}{\partial x_2}\frac{\partial x_2}{\partial p_2} + \frac{\partial S}{\partial p_2} + \frac{\partial x_1}{\partial p_2}\left[\frac{\partial S}{\partial x_1} + \frac{\partial S}{\partial x_2}\frac{\partial x_2}{\partial x_1}\right] = 0. \tag{1.4}$$

Alternatively, I can rewrite (1.1) as $p_1 = p_1(x_1, x_2)$ and $p_2 = p_2(x_1, x_2)$. Then, equivalent to (1.4), the FOC with respect to x_2 is rewritten as

$$\frac{\partial S}{\partial x_2} + \frac{\partial S}{\partial p_1}\frac{\partial p_1}{\partial x_2} + \frac{\partial S}{\partial p_2}\frac{\partial p_2}{\partial x_2} = 0. \tag{1.5}$$

This policy plan is optimal, but not the equilibrium. In equilibrium, the policy maker and agents make decisions at each time. In other words, they solve the problem sequentially. The FOC of **sequential policy (equilibrium policy)** with respect to p_2 is

$$\frac{\partial S}{\partial x_2}\frac{\partial x_2}{\partial p_2} + \frac{\partial S}{\partial p_2} = 0, \tag{1.6}$$

equivalently, the FOC with respect to x_2 is rewritten as

$$\frac{\partial S}{\partial x_2} + \frac{\partial S}{\partial p_2}\frac{\partial p_2}{\partial x_2} = 0. \tag{1.7}$$

When comparing (1.4) with (1.6), the third term of (1.4) disappears in (1.4). In the same manner, when comparing (1.5) with (1.7), the second term of (1.5) disappears in (1.7). In short, the sequential policy ignores the effect of the policy at $t = 2$ on the decision at $t = 1$. The reason is as follows: for the first best, the policy maker cares about the agents' decisions in both periods because that does not deviate from the initial plan. However, for the sequential policy, the policy maker deviates from the initial plan and ignores the past decisions.

In other words, these results mean that in the sequential decision, the first best policy is not carried out. Even if the policy maker announces the first best policy at the beginning of $t = 1$, it is not conducted when $t = 2$. The equilibrium satisfies (1.6). The equilibrium plan must consider the possibility of deviations. Then, the result is worse than the first best.

Kydland and Prescott (1977) take the example of the government flood control and people's house building. The government has flood control measures, and people seek places to build houses. In the optimal situation, people do not build houses in flood plain. Then, the government does not have to spend, and the people avoid the flood. However, people expect that if they build houses in a flood plain, where land price is low, the government would construct levees and dams to save them. Then, in the sequential equilibrium, this decision is chosen. This is worse than the first best.

In Chap. 2, I consider the relationship not between the consumer and the government but between the consumer and the firm. The monopolistic firm sets the price of the product, and consumers decide on the demand. I show that time inconsistency occurs in this relationship and prize promotions solve it.

1.2 Signaling

The signaling model is developed by Spence (1973, 1974). This model is categorized into the "incomplete information game" in which players' types are private information and other players do not know a player's type. Here, I introduce a signaling game for the job market and education. First, I briefly describe the structure of the signaling game. The signaling game is one type of dynamic incomplete information game. There are two players: sender and receiver. The sender has private information and sends a message (signal) to the receiver. After observing the signal, the receiver makes a decision. The detailed structure of the game is as follows:

1. Nature selects the type (t) of the sender. t obeys probabilistic distribution $p(t)$. The sender knows his/her type, but the receiver knows only $p(t)$.
2. The sender sends a signal (m) to the receiver.
3. The receiver observe m. He/she chooses action (a). His/her strategy is $a(m)$.

To find equilibria of the signaling game, I employ the concept of the "perfect Bayesian Equilibrium." The definition of a perfect Bayesian equilibrium is as follows:

Definition (*Perfect Bayesian Equilibrium*) Perfect Bayesian equilibrium in a signaling game are $m(t), a(m), andp(t|m)$ that satisfy the following conditions.

- The receiver has belief about the sender's type for each signal m. Under the belief, the receiver maximize his/her utility.
- The sender for each type, given the receiver's $a(m)$, maximizes his/her utility.
- For each signal m, the receiver creates a belief according to the Bayes' rule.

There can be **pooling equilibrium** and **separating equilibrium** in a signaling game. The pooling equilibrium refers to the case in which all senders send the same signals. The separating equilibrium refers to the case in which all senders send different signals.

Here, I take one example of the signaling game, job market signaling. The worker provides the firm with labor to gain wage, and firms employ workers to produce goods and gain profit. Here, the sender is workers, and the receiver is firms. In this environment, the types are workers' productivity, the signals are workers' education, and the action is wage payment. It is important to assume that education does not improve workers' productivity. For simplicity, firms are in a competitive environment, and profit is zero.

1. Nature selects the worker's type $t = l, h$, where $l < h$. The worker knows his/her type, but the firm only knows the probability distribution of t.
2. The worker chooses the education level $e = L, H$, where $L < H$.
3. The firm observes the education level e. It offers wage w to the worker.
4. The worker's gain $w - e/t$ and the firm's gain $t - w$ are determined.

Note that education does not improve workers' productivity. Education levels are only signals that firms can observe. In this model, which education level does each type of worker choose? Do both types of workers choose the same education level (i.e., pooling equilibrium)? Does each type of worker choose different education levels (i.e., separating equilibrium)? It can be shown that there is separating equilibrium in which the low ($t = l$) type chooses low education level ($e = L$), and the high ($t = h$) type chooses high education level ($e = H$). In short, even if education does not improve workers' productivity, people pay the cost of education to signal their hidden productivity.

References

Kydland, F., & Prescott, E. C. (1977). Rules rather than discretion: The inconsistency of optimal plans. *The Journal of Political Economy*, *85*(3), 473–492.
Spence, M. (1973). Job market signaling. *The Quarterly Journal of Economics*, *87*(3), 355–374.
Spence, M. (1974). *Market signalling*. Cambridge: Harvard University Press.

Chapter 2
Prize Promotions for Solving Firms' Time Inconsistency

Abstract Prize promotions have become extremely common in recent times. One such example is the "USD 100 present for 100 buyers" campaign. Prize promotions are known as firms' strategy to attract consumers and increase sales. This chapter sheds light on new aspect of prize promotions. I shows that prize promotions solve various time-inconsistency problems between firms and consumers; Consumers sometimes care about the number of users or popularization of the products in the future (e.g., video game devices). Consumers sometimes care about the increase in price of products they regularly purchase. In these cases, time inconsistency can occur: the firm would like to announce the future popularization of the products. However, the announcement of future popularization is not credible to the consumers. Then, current consumers do not purchase the goods. By employing prize promotions, the firm can credibly commit to future expansion of production. I also show when prize promotions are profitable.

Keywords Prize promotions · Advertisements · Time inconsistency

2.1 Introduction

Prize promotions are common especially in final goods market. One such example is the "USD 100 present for 100 buyers" campaign. Such prize promotions reflect a firm's policy of attaching a lottery ticket to each product. However, in a static economic model, attaching a lottery ticket is meaningless for the firm. It is equivalent to price cuts under risk-neutral preferences, since the firm is essentially paying back money to the consumers in the form of lottery tickets. Thus, if attaching lottery tickets does not play a unique role in the firm's strategy, then prize promotions can be considered unprofitable. However, this study shows that, in a dynamic environment, prize promotions not only imply price cuts but also serve as a commitment tool in resolving the time inconsistency between the firm and consumers. In more detail, prize promotions work equivalently to credible announcements even in the situation where credible announcements are unavailable.

M. Tamura, *Economic Signals*, Development Bank of Japan Research Series, https://doi.org/10.1007/978-981-10-8938-1_2

What is time inconsistency between the firm and consumers? One example appears in the market of video game devices. The maker of the video game device would like to announce that there will be many users of the device in the near future, because future popularization will attract current users and increase current profits. However, this type announcement is not credible to the consumers, as the maker has less incentive to increase users in the future than in the new-release period. As a result, consumers will not believe the announcement, and the maker cannot sufficiently increase the number of current users. This is one example of time inconsistency between the firm and consumers; in a sense, it is similar to the example seen in Kydland and Kydland and Prescott (1977). I theoretically show that prize promotions in general work to solve time inconsistency between the firm and consumers, including in this example.

This chapter is based on Tamura (2017), which makes three contributions to the literature. First, it highlights a new economic role of prize promotions: prize promotions are equivalent to costless credible announcements. Second, it proposes prize promotions as the best method for resolving time-inconsistency problems between firms and consumers in a general model. While various studies suggest solutions for mitigating the time-inconsistency problem and achieving the second-best outcome—including excess capacity (Dixit 1980), coupons (Cremer 1984), and second sourcing (Farrell and Gallini 1988)—prize promotions lead to the first-best result at no cost. Third, my model can be regarded as a new case in which the lottery is profitable under the risk-neutral preference. My study indicates how and when prize promotions (e.g., a lottery) are profitable in a dynamic model; it does so without considering asymmetric information (Milgrom and Roberts 1986) or any behavioral preference (Chew and Tan 2005).

There have been few studies to address the economic role of lotteries, sweepstakes, and prize promotions. Selby and Beranek (1981) prove that a lottery is unprofitable under risk-neutral and risk-averse preferences. Chew and Tan (2005) analyze the optimal price of a lottery under behavioral preferences and show that it is profitable. However, there has been no theoretical study of the present case, wherein a firm attaches a lottery ticket to its product. I show that such a lottery can be profitable, even in the absence of behavioral preferences. Kotler and Keller (2012) consider prize promotions as mere sales promotions that take the forms of coupons, cash refund offers, free trials, and/or product warranties. They suggest that sales promotions "*stimulate quicker or greater purchase of particular products.*" They do not explain why and how prize promotions stimulate product purchases, or the difference between prize promotions and price cuts. However, some empirical studies touch upon lotteries and prize promotions. Narayana and Raju (1985), for example, empirically test the effect of prize promotions on sales, and Kalra and Shi (2010) experimentally show how consumers value them.

The remainder of this chapter is organized as follows. Section 2.2 provides an example of time inconsistency. In Sect. 2.3, I introduce the general model where time inconsistency arises. In Sect. 2.4, I incorporate prize promotions into the model and solve the time-inconsistency problem. Section 2.5 interprets the results of my analysis. Section 2.6 solves a network externality model by using prize promotions. Section 2.6 concludes this chapter.

2.2 An Example of Time Inconsistency: Network Externality

I take an example of network externality. Network externality refers to cases in which each user's utility from the good positively depends on the number of users; examples include telecommunications, video games, software, and credit cards. For these goods, the existence of many users provides all users with many opportunities to play and communicate with other users and friends, and hence derive utility.

Firms that sell products with network externality (e.g., video game devices) sometimes face time inconsistency: users of video game devices hope that there will be many other users in the future. The more users there are, the more opportunities there are for the players to play with other players through the Internet, which yields much utility. The consumers' expectation of future popularization guarantees the consumers' utility from the devices, and induces both future and current sales. Then, the firm would like to announce future popularization of the devices. Is this announcement effective to attract many consumers and increase sales? The answer is no, because the announcement of future popularization is not credible to the consumers. The consumers are concerned that the firm would not be keen to sell the devices in the near future (i.e., it will cease making advertisements or introduce a new alternative device). The problem lies in the fact that the firm can freely change its policy from the initial announcement. The firm would like to make an announcement regarding future user expansion to attract current users and increase sales; however, this is not credible to the consumers. This is one example of time inconsistency between the firm and consumers.

Other types of goods also possess the property of network externality. The more users there are for an operating system or software, for example, the more help and information each user can draw from other users and the Internet. The more users there are for telecommunication, the more convenient it is to communicate with each other. For these goods, there can be time inconsistency between the firm and consumers. The firm would like to announce future popularization of such products, and attract many users. However, this announcement is not credible and results in lower sales.

2.3 Firm's Time Inconsistency in the General Two-Periods Model

2.3.1 The Model

Here, I describe the firm's inconsistency problem in a general model. Consider the following two-period sequential problem. In each period, the monopoly firm supplies the goods and the consumers demand them. The utility function and the budget constraint for consumer i are as follows:

$$U^i\left(x_1{}^i, x_2{}^i\right) = u^i\left(x_1{}^i, x_2{}^i\right) + M^i, \tag{2.1}$$

$$P_1 x_1{}^i + P_2 x_2{}^i + M^i = w^i, \tag{2.2}$$

where $U^i(\cdot)$ denotes consumer i's utility function, $u^i(\cdot)$ denotes i's utility from the good, $x_t{}^i$ denotes i's demand at time t, P_t denotes the price at time t, M^i denotes i's monetary gain, and w^i denotes i's income. Note that the utility function is quasi-linear in money, since I am considering prize promotions where the prize is given to consumers in the form of money.

The monopoly firm and consumers face sequential decisions. They do not make both current and future decisions at one point in time; they make only current decisions. In the model, at $t = 1$, the firm sets P_1, and consumer i decides $x_1{}^i$, given the current price P_1 and the future expected price P_2.[1] At $t = 2$, the firm sets P_2 and consumer i decides $x_2{}^i$, given the current price P_2 and past variables P_1 and $x_1{}^i$. This sequential problem can be regarded as a case in which the firm and consumers cannot credibly commit to their future decisions. In other words, the firm and consumers cannot make credible announcements regarding future decisions. They make discretionary decisions at each time.

Assuming interior solutions, the total demand functions for the good can be written as[2]

$$X_1 = \sum_i x_1{}^i\left(P_1, P_2\right), \tag{2.3}$$

$$X_2 = \sum_i x_2{}^i\left(P_2 \mid x_1{}^i\right), \tag{2.4}$$

where X_t denotes the total demand at time t. The profit of the monopoly firm is given by

$$\begin{aligned} \pi &= \pi_1 + \pi_2 \\ &= P_1 X_1 - C_1(X_1) + P_2 X_2 - C_2(X_2), \end{aligned} \tag{2.5}$$

where π denotes the total profit, π_t denotes the profit at time t, and $C_t(\cdot)$ denotes the cost function at time t. I assume that π_1 and π_2 are concave functions of X_1 and X_2, respectively.

[1] At the equilibrium, consumers rationally expect future price P_2.

[2] The demand does not depend on the past price, since the income effect is zero under quasi-linear utility.

2.3.2 With Credible Announcement

Before investigating the equilibrium, I need to undertake one type of normative analysis. Consider the hypothetical situation in which the firm can credibly commit to its future decision or make a credible announcement at $t = 1$. The firm at $t = 1$ announces its future decision and binds itself to following the announcement in the future. In other words, they can make both current and future decisions at $t = 1$. The firm's first-best policy is defined as follows:

Definition (*Firm's First-Best Policy*) The firm's *first-best* policy ($X_1{}^*$, $X_2{}^*$) solves

$$\max_{X_1, X_2} \pi. \tag{2.6}$$

Here, the firm maximizes the total profit as if it were facing a static problem. This ($X_1{}^*$, $X_2{}^*$) can be considered the *commitment equilibrium*, where the firm is able to make a credible commitment (announcement) regarding its current and future decisions. Focusing on the decision regarding X_2, for the first-best $X_2{}^*$, the FOC with respect to X_2 is

$$\frac{\partial \pi}{\partial X_2}(X_1{}^*, X_2) = \frac{\partial \pi_1}{\partial X_2}(X_1{}^*, X_2) + \frac{\partial \pi_2}{\partial X_2}(X_1{}^*, X_2) = 0. \tag{2.7}$$

2.3.3 Without Credible Announcement

Next, I return to the original setting of the model and investigate the equilibrium. I do not allow the firm to credibly commit to its future decisions. Instead, I consider the case in which the firm and consumers make decisions sequentially. In reality, many firms face sequential decisions and cannot make credible commitments with regard to their future policies (e.g., the firm's announcements themselves are costly, makers are unable to decide on future retail prices, or the firm can easily deviate from the announcement). The firm decides P_1 and X_1 at $t = 1$ and P_2 and X_2 at $t = 2$. Therefore, if the firm initially makes an announcement, generally speaking, it will not be credible to the consumers. The firm can deviate from it discretionally. Suppose $X_1 = X_1{}^*$. I focus on the sequential decision regarding X_2 at $t = 2$. The sequential decision solves

$$\max_{X_2} \pi_2. \tag{2.8}$$

For the sequential decision, the FOC with respect to X_2 is

$$\frac{\partial \pi_2}{\partial X_2}(X_1{}^*, X_2) = 0. \tag{2.9}$$

Note that the difference between this sequential FOC (2.9) and the first-best FOC (2.7) lies in the term $\frac{\partial \pi_1}{\partial X_2}(X_1{}^*, X_2)$. In other words, the sequential problem and the first-best problem yield different solutions, under the condition of

$$\frac{\partial \pi_1}{\partial X_2}(X_1{}^*, X_2{}^*) \neq 0. \tag{2.10}$$

In this case, I say that the first-best policy is *time inconsistent.*

Definition (*Time Inconsistency*) If the firm's first-best policy $(X_1{}^*, X_2{}^*)$ is the same as the solution to the sequential problem, I say that $(X_1{}^*, X_2{}^*)$ is time consistent. On the other hand, if the firm's first-best policy $(X_1{}^*, X_2{}^*)$ is not the same as the solution to the sequential problem, I say that $(X_1{}^*, X_2{}^*)$ is time inconsistent.

In other words, time inconsistency arises when the decision with a credible announcement is not carried out in the sequential problem without a credible announcement. Suppose that the firm initially announces the first-best policy $(X_1{}^*, X_2{}^*)$ at $t = 1$. Time inconsistency matters if, at $t = 2$, the firm has an incentive to deviate from the initial announcement $X_2{}^*$. In this case, the firm's initial announcement is not credible to the consumers and the first best is not the equilibrium. In the real economy, the firm sometimes faces the decision that acts contrary to the previous consumers' expectations: suppose X_1 is printer and X_2 is ink. After the printers are sold, the firm raises the price (equivalently, reduces the quantity) of ink. Suppose X_1 is lifts and X_2 is lift maintenance. After the lifts are sold, the firm increases the maintenance fee (equivalently, reduces the quantity). If the initial first-best announcement is not credible and not the equilibrium, the actual equilibrium is another decision that yields a profit lower than the first-best policy would. In contrast, a *time-consistent* policy is one for which the firm has no incentive to deviate from the initial announcement in the sequential problem; that is, the sequential decision is equal to the first best. Note that the meaning of the term "inconsistency" is as implied by Kydland and Prescott (1977), where the government (central bank) is said to have an incentive to deviate from an initial announcement in monetary policy.

Time inconsistency arises when the firm cannot credibly commit to the future policy—that is, if there is time inconsistency, then credible commitment is required to implement the first-best decision. In this case, I consider the following question: what type of credible commitment is required for the first-best decision? The answer depends on the demand function. As seen above, the difference between the first-best FOC (2.7) and the sequential FOC (2.9) is the term $\frac{\partial \pi_1}{\partial X_2}(X_1{}^*, X_2)$, which is rewritten as $\frac{\partial P_1}{\partial X_2}(X_1{}^*, X_2)X_1{}^*$.

Definition (*Required Type of Commitment*) If (2.11) holds, then I say that expansionary commitment is required for the first best.

$$\frac{\partial \pi_1}{\partial X_2}(X_1{}^*, X_2{}^*) = \frac{\partial P_1}{\partial X_2}(X_1{}^*, X_2{}^*)X_1{}^* > 0 \tag{2.11}$$

Conversely, if (2.12) holds, then I say that contractionary commitment is required for the first best.

$$\frac{\partial \pi_1}{\partial X_2}(X_1{}^*, X_2{}^*) = \frac{\partial P_1}{\partial X_2}(X_1{}^*, X_2{}^*)X_1{}^* < 0 \tag{2.12}$$

The above definitions are derived from the following. If (2.11) holds, the sequential FOC (2.9) results in a lower X_2, relative to that derived with the first-best FOC (2.7). If (2.12) holds, the sequential FOC (2.9) results in higher X_2, relative to that derived with the first-best FOC (2.7).

In addition, it should be noted that expansionary commitment is equivalent to a price reduction commitment. Since the firm is assumed to be a monopoly, quantity expansion implies price declines if the demand functions are decreasing in the current price. Thus, the definition can be restated as follows. *If* (2.11) *holds, I say that the price reduction commitment is required for the first best. Conversely, if* (2.12) *holds, I say that the price rise commitment is required for the first best.*

This model can be regarded as a generalization of various other models that consider switching costs (Farrell and Gallini 1988), experience goods (Cremer 1984), and network externality, as I discuss in Sect. 2.6. For instance, consider a model of switching costs. At times, consumers need to pay switching or adoption costs for using goods (e.g., printer/ink or elevator/maintenance fees). Consumers purchase goods at both $t = 1$ and $t = 2$. However, at $t = 1$, they have to additionally pay large switching (adoption) costs in order to use and derive utility from the goods. Switching costs serve as entrance fees for the goods. Consumers' entry decisions at $t = 1$ will clearly depend on the future pricing of goods by the firm. If consumers expect that the firm will increase prices in the future, then they will not pay entrance fees (switching costs) and not purchase the goods. This situation corresponds to (2.11), and so expansionary (price reduction) commitment is required for the first-best. In Sect. 2.6, network externality is considered as an example.

2.4 Prize Promotions: A Solution to Inconsistency

I have shown that in the sequential decision, the firm cannot make a credible future announcement, and the first best is not carried out. Then, I suggest prize promotions as a commitment tool in the sequential decision. Although prize promotions are not simple announcements on the surface, they work in the same manner as costless credible announcements.

The firm attaches a lottery ticket to each product at both $t = 1$ and $t = 2$. The lottery prize is money, and the total prize amount is announced and fixed at the beginning of $t = 1$.[3] At the end of $t = 2$, one or more winning tickets are randomly

[3] I implicitly assume that the firm can announce and commit to the prize amount at $t = 1$. This assumption is reasonable, as deviation from the announcement would violate commercial laws in many countries.

selected by draw. It should be noted that the winning tickets are selected from among all the tickets supplied in both time periods. For simplicity, I also assume that the consumers are atomless—for each consumer i, the aggregate variable $X_t \equiv \sum_i x_t{}^i$ is given. The aggregate demand for the good is determined by

$$X_1 = \sum_i x_1{}^i\left(P_1 - \frac{Prize}{X_1 + X_2}, P_2 - \frac{Prize}{X_1 + X_2}\right), \tag{2.13}$$

$$X_2 = \sum_i x_2{}^i\left(P_2 - \frac{Prize}{X_1 + X_2} \,\middle|\, x_1{}^i\right), \tag{2.14}$$

where $Prize$ denotes the total prize amount. Because $\frac{Prize}{X_1+X_2}$ represents the value of one lottery ticket, $P_t - \frac{Prize}{X_1+X_2}$ can be interpreted as the real price of the good itself. The firm's profit is

$$\begin{aligned}\pi &= \pi_1 + \pi_2 - Prize \\ &= P_1X_1 - C_1(X_1) + P_2X_2 - C_2(X_2) - Prize.\end{aligned} \tag{2.15}$$

Note that $Prize$ is a cost for the firm, since it must pay $Prize$ to the consumers at the end of $t = 2$. Here, I derive the main proposition of this study.

Proposition (Costless Commitment by Prize Promotions) *Consider a two-period sequential model where*

(i) the atomless consumers' demand functions are (2.3) and (2.4), and
(ii) the monopoly firm's profit function is (2.5); π_1 and π_2 are concave functions of X_1 and X_2.

If expansionary (price reduction) commitment is required for the time inconsistent the first best $X_1{}^*$ and $X_2{}^*$, the following firm policy makes $X_1{}^*$ and $X_2{}^*$ time consistent and yields the first-best profit:

$$\begin{cases} P_1 = P_1\left(X_1{}^*, X_2{}^* | Prize = 0\right) + \dfrac{Prize}{X_1{}^* + X_2{}^*}, & (2.16) \\ P_2 = P_2\left(X_1{}^*, X_2{}^* | Prize = 0\right) + \dfrac{Prize}{X_1{}^* + X_2{}^*}, & (2.17) \\ Prize = (X_1{}^* + X_2{}^*)^2 \dfrac{\partial P_1}{\partial X_2}(X_1{}^*, X_2{}^*), & (2.18) \end{cases}$$

where $P_t\left(X_1, X_2 | Prize = 0\right)$ denotes the inverse demand function at time t when $Prize = 0$.

Proof Let $P_1\big(X_1, X_2|Prize = 0\big)$ and $P_2\big(X_1, X_2|Prize = 0\big)$ denote the inverse demand functions at $t = 1$ and $t = 2$ when $Prize = 0$. Thus,

$$P_1(X_1, X_2) = P_1\big(X_1, X_2|Prize = 0\big) + \frac{Prize}{X_1 + X_2}, \; and \tag{2.19}$$

$$P_2(X_1, X_2) = P_2\big(X_1, X_2|Prize = 0\big) + \frac{Prize}{X_1 + X_2}, \tag{2.20}$$

are the inverse demand functions when $Prize > 0$, because the pricing policy $(P_1, P_2) = \big(P_1(X_1, X_2), P_2(X_1, X_2)\big)$ clearly yields demands X_1 and X_2.

Next, let us check for consistency. Suppose that $X_1 = X_1{}^*$. The first-best FOC (2.7) can be written as

$$\begin{aligned}\frac{\partial \pi}{\partial X_2}(X_1{}^*, X_2) &= \frac{\partial \pi_1}{\partial X_2}(X_1{}^*, X_2) + \frac{\partial \pi_2}{\partial X_2}(X_1{}^*, X_2)\\ &= \frac{\partial\Big(P_1\big(X_1{}^*, X_2|Prize = 0\big)X_1{}^* - C_1(X_1{}^*)\Big)}{\partial X_2}\\ &\quad + \frac{\partial\Big(P_2\big(X_1{}^*, X_2|Prize = 0\big)X_2 - C_2(X_2)\Big)}{\partial X_2}\\ &= 0.\end{aligned} \tag{2.21}$$

When $Prize = 0$, the sequential FOC (2.9) is $\frac{\partial \pi_2}{\partial X_2}(X_1{}^*, X_2) = \frac{\partial\left(P_2\left(X_1{}^*, X_2|Prize=0\right)X_2 - C_2(X_2)\right)}{\partial X_2} = 0$. However, when $Prize > 0$, the sequential FOC becomes

$$\begin{aligned}\frac{\partial \pi_2}{\partial X_2}(X_1{}^*, X_2) &= \frac{\partial\Big(\Big(P_2\big(X_1{}^*, X_2|Prize = 0\big) + \frac{Prize}{X_1{}^* + X_2}\Big)X_2 - C_2(X_2)\Big)}{\partial X_2}\\ &= \frac{\partial\Big(P_2\big(X_1{}^*, X_2|Prize = 0\big)X_2 - C_2(X_2)\Big)}{\partial X_2} + \frac{\partial \frac{Prize}{X_1{}^* + X_2}X_2}{\partial X_2}\\ &= 0.\end{aligned} \tag{2.22}$$

The sequential FOC (2.22) is the same as the first-best FOC (2.21) by setting $\frac{\partial \frac{Prize}{X_1{}^* + X_2}X_2}{\partial X_2} = \frac{\partial\left(P_1\left(X_1{}^*, X_2|Prize=0\right)X_1{}^* - C_1(X_1{}^*)\right)}{\partial X_2}$ at $X_2 = X_2{}^*$; equivalently,

$$Prize = (X_1{}^* + X_2{}^*)^2 \frac{\partial P_1}{\partial X_2}(X_1{}^*, X_2{}^*). \tag{2.23}$$

Therefore, the firm's policy

$$\begin{cases} P_1 = P_1\left(X_1{}^*, X_2{}^* | Prize = 0\right) + \dfrac{Prize}{X_1{}^* + X_2{}^*}, & (2.24) \\ P_2 = P_2\left(X_1{}^*, X_2{}^* | Prize = 0\right) + \dfrac{Prize}{X_1{}^* + X_2{}^*}, & (2.25) \\ Prize = (X_1{}^* + X_2{}^*)^2 \dfrac{\partial P_1}{\partial X_2}(X_1{}^*, X_2{}^*), & (2.26) \end{cases}$$

yields $X_1 = X_1{}^*$ and $X_2 = X_2{}^*$, which is time-consistent. Moreover, if $\frac{\partial P_1}{\partial X_2}(X_1{}^*, X_2{}^*) > 0$ (defined earlier as "expansionary commitment is required"), then there exists a positive value for $Prize = (X_1{}^* + X_2{}^*)^2 \frac{\partial P_1}{\partial X_2}(X_1{}^*, X_2{}^*)$.

Finally, I consider the profit resulting from the firm's policy, as discussed above. The total profit does not depend on $Prize$, but on X_1 and X_2, because

$$\begin{aligned} \pi &= \pi_1 + \pi_2 - Prize \\ &= \left(P_1\left(X_1, X_2 | Prize = 0\right) + \frac{Prize}{X_1 + X_2}\right) X_1 - C(X_1) \\ &\quad + \left(P_2\left(X_1, X_2 | Prize = 0\right) + \frac{Prize}{X_1 + X_2}\right) X_2 - C(X_2) - Prize \\ &= P_1\left(X_1, X_2 | Prize = 0\right) X_1 - C(X_1) + P_2\left(X_1, X_2 | Prize = 0\right) X_2 - C(X_2). \end{aligned} \tag{2.27}$$

Therefore, the firm's policy, as discussed above, yields the first-best profit. □

This proposition states that by controlling the amount of $Prize$, the firm can bind itself to not deviate from the initial announcement. In addition, the prize promotions are costless, since the firm can make the first-best profit. Thus, the prize promotions are equivalent to costless credible announcements. In the next section, I interpret the above proposition.

2.5 Interpretations

2.5.1 *Theoretical Interpretations*

If the firm does not use prize promotions, π_2 is simply represented as $\pi_2 = P_2\left(X_1{}^*, X_2 \mid Prize = 0\right) X_2 - C(X_2)$ in the sequential problem. On the other hand, if the firm uses prize promotions (as seen in (2.22)), π_2 becomes

$$\pi_2 = \underbrace{P_2\Big(X_1{}^*, X_2 \mid Prize = 0\Big)X_2 - C(X_2)}_{Prize=0} + \underbrace{\frac{Prize}{X_1{}^* + X_2}X_2}_{Prize>0}. \tag{2.28}$$

In short, if the firm sets $Prize > 0$, the last term appears in the maximization problem at $t = 2$. Since $\frac{Prize}{X_1{}^*+X_2}$ is the value of one lottery ticket, the last term $\frac{Prize}{X_1{}^*+X_2}X_2$ represents **the value of all the tickets held by the consumers at t = 2**.

- Why is this value an increasing function of X_2?

The higher the number of lottery tickets distributed by the firm at t $= 2$, *the higher is the probability of winners at t* $= 2$ *and the lower is the probability of winners at t* $= 1$. *Thus, by printing more tickets at t* $= 2$, *the firm can shift the prize winners from t* $= 1$ *to t* $= 2$.

- Why does this value appear in π_2?

Irrespective of the number of tickets distributed by the firm at t $= 2$, *the prize cost (i.e., total prize amount) is considered a sunk cost, since it was already announced and fixed at t* $= 1$. *Thus, at t* $= 2$, *the firm considers only the benefit from the prize and not the cost—that is, it considers the value of all the tickets held by the consumers at t* $= 2$.

To summarize, at $t = 2$, printing more tickets allows the firm to reward the consumers at $t = 2$ more and make greater profits, all without needing to make any additional prize payment. Thus, in the future, the firm will expand production along with lottery tickets. The firm, by making announcements on prize promotions at $t = 1$, informs the consumers that it will be undertaking production expansion in the future in order to distribute more lottery tickets.

2.5.2 Effective and Ineffective Prize Promotions

Next, I distinguish between effective and ineffective prize promotions. There are two types of prize promotions.

(i) Fixed Prize Funds.
For example,

- USD 100 for 100 buyers, and
- one automobile for one buyer.

(ii) Variable Prize Funds.
For example,

- USD 100 cash back for 1% of the consumers, and
- USD 1 cash back for every purchase.

In the type (i) example of "USD 100 for 100 buyers," the prize funds do not depend on sales and are fixed at a total of USD 10,000. In the type (ii) example of "USD 100 cash back for 1% of the consumers," the prize funds depend on sales. I have showed that type (i) is effective and resolves the inconsistency problem. However, is this true for type (ii) as well? I conclude that type (ii) is ineffective and does not resolve the inconsistency problem for the following reason. At $t = 2$, to give more prizes to the current consumers, the firm needs to distribute more lottery tickets, which leads to the firm's additional prize payment. The total prize amount for the latter type increases with the number of tickets. In short, with this type of prize promotion, the prize fund is not a sunk cost, and so the firm does not have any incentive to distribute more lottery tickets at $t = 2$.

2.5.3 *Prize Promotions in an Oligopoly Model*

Firms' time-inconsistency problems are divided into two categories. The first category pertains to the strategic relationships among firms. In the oligopoly model, the firm tries to announce the future plan to other firms (Dixit 1980). The second category pertains to the relationship between the firm and consumers. The firm tries to announce the future plan to consumers in the monopoly model (Cremer 1984, Farrell and Gallini 1988). The first category focuses on strategic relationships, and the second category focuses on nonstrategic relationships. My model is in the second category, as I analyze the firm and consumers' repeat buying; this study ignores the strategic aspect.

So far, I have shown that prize promotions solve the second category. Then, I would like to examine briefly whether or not prize promotions solve the first "strategic" category. My answer is that prize promotions can also solve inconsistency among firms, though I cannot say that they are always the best (i.e., costless) tool to solve it. As an example, I consider a variation of the Dixit (1980) two-period model: at $t = 1$, a monopolistic firm (incumbent) supplies goods and announces the production plan in the next period. At the beginning of $t = 2$, the follower decides whether or not to enter the market. There are two subgames. (1) If the follower enters the market in the hope of a positive profit, at $t = 2$, the incumbent and follower play a Cournot game. (2) Otherwise, at $t = 2$, the incumbent supplies goods as the monopoly firm. (Note that consumers' demand is time independent.) In this case, at $t = 1$, the incumbent would like to deter the follower's entry and announce future production expansion to warn that the follower does not gain a positive profit after the entry. However, the incumbent's announcement is both not credible and time inconsistent, because the incumbent's threat of future production expansion would not be carried out if the follower were to actually enter the market and play a Cournot game.

Dixit (1980) proposes investment at $t = 1$ for the incumbent's announcement to be a credible threat. An example of the investment is establishing a new factory in the manufacturing industry. Establishing a new factory means that the firm is going to expand future production. If the incumbent pays for investment that is a sunk cost and changes the profitability, the investment works as a credible announcement of future production expansion and deters the follower's entry, hence solving time inconsistency among firms. On the other hand, how do prize promotions work in the Dixit (1980) model? Prize promotions also work effectively because expansionary commitment is required and the firm is the price maker, even in this oligopoly model. At $t = 1$, the incumbent attaches a lottery ticket to each product at both $t = 1$ and $t = 2$. The total amount of prize is announced at the beginning of $t = 1$, and winning tickets are selected at the end of $t = 2$. Then, if the follower were to enter the market, the incumbent would expand the production in the Cournot competition. As a result, the incumbent can credibly commit to future production expansion and deter the follower's entry.

It should be noted that the prize promotions do not lead to the first-best profit. In other words, prize promotions are not equivalent to a credible announcement. This is because prize promotions affect both subgames (1) and (2) together, while a credible announcement can affect only subgame (1). Prize promotions end up distorting the optimization problem in subgame (2), which leads to profits lower than those seen with a credible announcement. Which is better: investment or prize promotions? I cannot answer this as the cost of investment is undefined. Therefore, while I conclude that prize promotions also work effectively in strategic situations, I cannot say that they are always the best tool.

2.6 Prize Promotions Solve the Example of Network Externality

In this section, by applying the main theorem of this chapter, I show that prize promotions solve the time-inconsistency problem introduced above as an example. I consider a two-generation network externality model that is largely based on Katz and Shapiro (1986) model. The structure of the example model is as follows. There are two time periods, two generations of consumers, and one monopoly firm that sells a durable good (video game device) with network externality. Generation 1 consumers live from $t = 1$ to $t = 2$. If generation 1 buys the devices only at $t = 1$, it can derive utility at both $t = 1$ and $t = 2$, because video games are durable goods. Generation 2 consumers live in $t = 2$. They enter the economy at $t = 2$ and buy the devices only at $t = 2$.

Their respective utility functions are

$$\text{Generation } 1: U^i = u^i\left(x^i, X_1\right) + u^i\left(x^i, X_1 + X_2\right), \tag{2.29}$$

$$\text{Generation } 2: U^i = u^i\left(x^i, X_1 + X_2\right). \tag{2.30}$$

Note that the total amount of goods has a positive effect on each good's owner; that is, $u^i(\cdot)$ is an increasing function of X_1 and $X_1 + X_2$.

Thus, the demand functions are

$$X_1 = \sum_i x_1\Big(P_1, X_1, X_1 + X_2\Big), \tag{2.31}$$

$$X_2 = \sum_i x_2\Big(P_2, X_1 + X_2 \mid X_1\Big). \tag{2.32}$$

Here, X_2 can be rewritten as $X_2 = X_2\big(P_2 \mid X_1\big)$; hence, $X_1 = X_1\big(P_1, P_2\big)$. These demand functions take the same form of (2.3) and (2.4). The firm's profit is

$$\begin{aligned}\pi &= \pi_1 + \pi_2 \\ &= P_1X_1 - C_1(X_1) + P_2X_2 - C_2(X_2),\end{aligned} \tag{2.33}$$

which is the same as (2.5). Moreover, from (2.31), it is clear that $\frac{\partial \pi_1}{\partial X_2}(X_1{}^*, X_2{}^*) = \frac{\partial P_1}{\partial X_2}(X_1{}^*, X_2{}^*)X_1{}^* > 0$, which was defined earlier as "expansionary commitment is required." Intuitively, for the sequential decision at $t = 2$, the firm has an incentive to deviate from the first-best policy; it reduces the supplies because it does not focus on the positive externality from X_2 to the consumers at $t = 1$. Since all the conditions satisfy the assumptions, I can apply the proposition to this model. Prize promotions work to implement the first best.

2.7 Concluding Remarks

Considering firms' static problems, theoretically, prize promotions are not profitable, as they are equivalent to price cuts. Thus, prize promotions are mere sales promotions. However, I show that, in the context of firms' dynamic problems, prize promotions are profitable, since they resolve a firm's time-inconsistency problems. It is to be emphasized that prize promotions are the best commitment tool for a firm, in the sense that they are equivalent to a costless credible announcement regarding the firm's future policy: with them, a firm can implement the first-best commitment equilibrium.

Prize promotions work as costless credible commitments to future production expansion for the following reasons. First, commitments to future expansion are a result of the dynamic nature of a lottery. By controlling the number of newly issued lottery tickets, the lottery seller (the firm) can change the value of not only the newly issued tickets but also that of the old tickets. Thus, the seller has an incentive to print more tickets in the future. Second, prize promotions are costless because, in one aspect, they can be regarded as a pricing strategy. As discussed above, even in a static environment, prize promotions are equivalent to price discounts for both the firm and consumers. Therefore, prize promotions are not an additional cost but a costless advertisement for a firm.

Various other ways of dealing with time inconsistency between firms and consumers have been suggested to achieve what is known as the second best. For example, Dixit (1980) suggests excess capacity, while Farrell and Gallini 1988 suggest second sourcing. Excess capacity may be an entry barrier; however, the firm has to make an investment in advance and maintain it for a certain period, and this represents an additional cost for the firm. Farrell and Gallini (1988) describe second sourcing as "*voluntarily inviting competitors into the market, usually by licensing a product at low royalties or by using an 'open architecture'* ". At times, second sourcing can increase profits, but the firm must relinquish its patents, and hence its monopoly power. this leads only to the second best, which is naturally worse than the first best. Thus, prize promotions are costless and better than these methods if the firm needs to make an expansionary (or price reduction) commitment.

References

Chew, S. H., & Tan, G. (2005). The market for sweepstakes. *The Review of Economic Studies, 72*(4), 1009–1029.

Cremer, J. (1984). On the economics of repeat buying. *The Rand Journal of Economics, 15*(3), 396–403.

Dixit, A. (1980). The role of investment in entry deterrence. *The Economic Journal, 90*(357), 95–106.

Farrell, J., & Gallini, N. T. (1988). Second-sourcing as a commitment: Monopoly incentives to attract competition. *The Quarterly Journal of Economics, 103*(4), 673–694.

Kalra, A., & Shi, M. (2010). Consumer value-maximizing sweepstakes and contests. *Journal of Marketing Research, 47*(2), 287–300.

Katz, M. L., & Shapiro, C. (1986). Technology adoption in the presence of network externalities. *The Journal of Political Economy, 94*(4), 822–841.

Kotler, P., & Keller, K. L. (2012). *Marketing management* (14th ed.). New Jersey: Pearson.

Kydland, F., & Prescott, E. C. (1977). Rules rather than discretion: The inconsistency of optimal plans. *The Journal of Political Economy, 85*(3), 473–492.

Milgrom, P., & Roberts, J. (1986). Price and advertising signals of product quality. *The Journal of Political Economy, 94*(4), 796–821.

Narayana, C. L., & Raju, P. S. (1985). Gifts versus sweepstakes: Consumer choices and profiles. *Journal of Advertising, 14*(1), 50–53.

Selby, E, Jr., & Beranek, W. B. (1981). Sweepstakes contests: Analysis, strategies, and survey. *The American Economic Review, 71*(1), 189–195.

Tamura, M. (2016). Prize promotions as costless commitments. *Managerial and Decision Economics, 38*(4), 556–564.

Chapter 3
Giving and Anonymous Giving for Signaling

Abstract Though some donors boast about their giving, others do not make their giving public. The former behavior is called known giving and the latter is called anonymous giving. Is anonymous giving really a virtue as is generally recognized? Paradoxically, this chapter proves that anonymity is a vice for fundraisers even if it is what donors desire. Existence of anonymous donors can impair others' incentive to give. In my signaling model, people's altruism is private information, and unobservable to others. By giving, people signal their hidden altruism to gain good reputation. I assume that people have image motivation in the sense that reputation (social image) yields utility. Practically, fundraisers should control the number of anonymous donors to increase the total amount of giving. Fundraisers often provide "check boxes" on their Web site to make it convenient to donate anonymously. I suggest that fundraisers should remove the check boxes from their Web sites.

Keywords Anonymous giving · Image motivation · Signaling

3.1 Introduction

People have two motivations for giving. The first motivation is altruism. They care about disadvantaged children, countries in need, and social fairness. Giving to solve these problems directly yields utility to them. Conversely, I can say that altruists give. The second motivation is altruistic social image. People want to be seen as altruistic by others, because altruism is a virtue in society. By giving, people are seen as altruists and gain a good social image. In this sense, giving also indirectly yields utility to them. From this point of view, even if people are not altruists and not really interested in disadvantaged children, they pretend to be altruists and give to social causes. I see situations wherein some celebrities' charity activities are criticized as self-advertisement and not altruism. This is because this giving may come from the second motivation. They possibly pretend to be altruists to gain a good social image.

For fundraisers, both motivations are important, because, not motivation but the total amount of giving is the objective of fundraising. To solicit significant funds, fundraisers have to satisfy both motivations of donors as much as they can. Especially,

M. Tamura, *Economic Signals*, Development Bank of Japan Research Series, https://doi.org/10.1007/978-981-10-8938-1_3

for donors' image motivation, they publish the donors' names, and send stickers or guarantees of giving to the donors. Then, donors can show their own altruistic image to others. In short, fundraisers enhance the reputation of giving to attract more giving.

Here, I pay attention to one specific type of giving, anonymous giving. Though some donors boast about their giving, others do not make their giving public. The former behavior is called known giving and the latter is called anonymous giving. While known giving results from the first, second, or both motivations, anonymous giving clearly results from the first motivation, altruism. Anonymous donors are not motivated by the second motivation, social image, because their giving is, by definition, not revealed to others. Therefore, in the common sense, anonymous giving is considered as altruistic and, hence, a virtue. In this sense, social image of known giving is not better than anonymous giving.

What is the relationship between known giving and anonymous giving? Whichever donors choose, does it make no difference for fundraisers? This chapter points out that anonymous giving sometimes decreases the total amount of giving, though anonymous giving is commonly seen as a virtue. The existence of anonymous giving affects the image of known giving. For example, if many other givings in society were made anonymously, then celebrities' charitable activities (known giving) would receive more criticism, and celebrities would cease to make known giving. In this case, by known giving, celebrities fail to pretend to be altruists, because many altruists choose anonymous giving. In this chapter, by using the model, I view this negative side of anonymous giving.

Practically, fundraisers should control the expected number of anonymous donors. However, I can find one example that exaggerates the existence of anonymous donors. Currently, many fundraisers solicit contributions via the Internet in addition to normal fundraising activities. On their Web sites, some fundraisers place check boxes for donors to select anonymous or known donations. Figure 3.1 shows how such a typical Web site looks. On the page, donors fill out not only information about the amount of donation, name, address, and credit card number but also the check box "*I prefer to make this donation anonymously*." By providing the check boxes, these fundraisers intend to make it convenient to donate anonymously. The problem, however, is that when facing the choice, donors assume that fundraisers provided the check box in response to many requests from a substantial number of anonymous donors. In other words, the check box exaggerates the number of anonymous donors.

Many studies, including Andreoni and Petrie (2004), Rege and Telle (2004), and Soetevent (2005), show that if experimenters control the anonymity of examinees, the examinees change their prosocial behavior. The more anonymity experimenters provide, the less altruistic the examinees become. A novel feature of this study is that anonymity is determined by the donors themselves. While some donors boast about their giving, others give anonymously. Is anonymous giving worth the same as known giving to fundraisers? Is anonymous giving really a virtue, as is generally recognized? Paradoxically, this study proves that anonymous giving is a vice, even if the donors themselves desire anonymity.

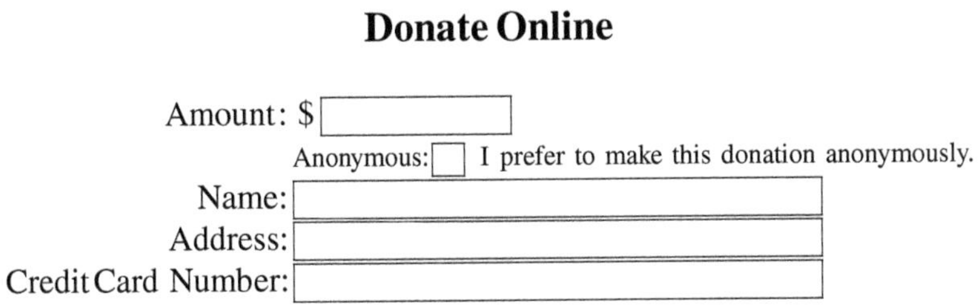

Fig. 3.1 Online donation page

This chapter is based on Tamura (2012). It extends Benabou and Tirole (2006) image signaling framework to the case in which "anonymity" is redefined and individuals themselves choose the anonymity level. Since people care about their social reputations, even non-altruists donate to conceal their selfishness and enhance their reputations. The key lies in this "hypocritical" behavior of donors. Such behavior is possible because altruism is private information and the donation amount is what others observe; giving enables non-altruists to mimic altruists and achieve recognition as altruists. However, if I allow donors the option of anonymous giving, it is clear that not all donors will choose the same anonymity level. It is essential to identify who donates anonymously, because it determines whether anonymous giving is independent of or related to the hypocritical behavior. The result shows that those who prefer anonymous giving are the best "target" for non-altruists to mimic, and the existence of anonymous donors negatively affects the hypocritical behavior of non-altruists and the total amount of donation.

The contribution of this study is threefold. First and foremost, it suggests how fundraising campaigns can be more efficiently designed: fundraisers should allow anonymous donation only as an exception and should not exaggerate the number of anonymous donors. Specifically, I can identify inefficiency in some fundraising Web sites and suggest an improvement. Such sites can impose a small "foot cost" on anonymous giving. Second, this is the first study that examines a model in which anonymity is endogenously determined. Here, anonymity is controlled not by the fundraisers but by donors themselves. Thus, I can study the case in which donors choose perfect anonymity, namely, by donating anonymously; almost no economic studies have addressed this case in detail. Third, the study gives weight to the heterogeneity of image motivation among individuals, in contrast to Benabou and Tirole (2006). Thus, I can identify who donates anonymously.

The remainder of this chapter is organized as follows. Section 3.2 provides the structure of the model. Section 3.3 briefly describes the main points of the model. Section 3.4 solves the model and investigate the equilibrium. In Sect. 3.5, I take an example of fundraisers' Web sites and draw policy implications.

3.2 Structure of the Model

People have two motivations for giving. The first motivation is altruism, and the second is image motivation.[1] Altruism means that giving itself yields utility for donors. Image motivation means that the reputation of altruism yields utility for donors.

The main characteristics and assumptions of my model are as follows: (1) Individuals derive utility directly from private goods, giving, and reputation of altruism. (2) There are two-dimensional heterogeneities in individual's preference parameters: altruism (selfishness) and self-consciousness about their own reputations. (3) Because these two parameters are private information and unobservable to others, individuals form beliefs about others' parameters of altruism (i.e., the reputation of altruism) based on the observable variables. (4) The other variables, including the giving amount, are perfectly observable. The key is that the existence of anonymous donors affects the group image of both known donors and non-donors.

The utility function that includes these two motivations is

$$U(c_i, x_i, \hat{\alpha}_i) = (1 - \alpha_i) \ln c_i + \alpha_i \ln x_i + \beta_i \ln I(\hat{\alpha}_i). \tag{3.1}$$

Here, c_i denotes individual i's consumption for private goods, x_i denotes individual i's donation, α_i denotes the altruism parameter, and β_i denotes the self-consciousness of individual i. Individuals are heterogeneous in parameters α_i and β_i. Because I assume that individual i's parameters α_i and β_i are private information and unobservable to all other individuals, others form beliefs about i's parameters. $\hat{\alpha}_i$ denotes the belief of other individuals about i's altruism, α_i. Individuals derive utility directly from this belief of others, namely, the extent to which others consider an individual altruistic. This corresponds to the concept of self-image or image motivation. The function $I(\cdot)$ represents this image motivation of individuals. I assume that $I'(\cdot) > 0$ and that $I(0) = 1$. People who are considered socially altruistic have a high $\hat{\alpha}_i$ and hence high utility. The more altruistic they are considered, the more utility they gain. Here, the heterogeneity lies in altruism α_i and self-consciousness β_i, which I specify below.

The budget constraint for i is

$$c_i + x_i = y_i, \tag{3.2}$$

$$x_i = D_i x_{ki} + (1 - D_i) x_{ai}. \tag{3.3}$$

Here, y_i is the endowment of individual i. People allocate their income between consumption and donation. x_k is known donation, x_a is anonymous donation, and D_i is a dummy variable that takes the value of 1 if individual i chooses known over

[1] Theoretical and empirical backgrounds for these two motivations are given in Andreoni (1989, 1990), Ariely et al. (2009), Benabou and Tirole (2006), Carpenter and Myers (2010), Crumpler and Grossman (2008), and Palfrey and Prisbrey (1997).

anonymous donation, and takes the value of 0 if individual i chooses anonymous over known donation. In short, in this model, when individuals want to donate, they must choose between a known and an anonymous donation. For simplicity, I assume that individuals cannot make both anonymous and known donations at the same time. I must draw attention to the implied assumption that the choice between anonymous and known donation does not directly affect the utility: both choices yield the same warm-glow utility. However, the choice does matter when individuals form beliefs about others' α values: $\hat{\alpha_i}$. $\hat{\alpha_i}$ is formed by

$$\hat{\alpha_i} = E[\alpha_i | \boldsymbol{x_k}], \tag{3.4}$$

where $\boldsymbol{x_k} \equiv \{x_{k1}, x_{k2}, ..., x_{kn}\}$. In words, $\boldsymbol{x_k}$ denotes the amount of known giving for all individuals in the economy. Equation (3.4) claims that beliefs about others' altruism are formed based on known donation. In other words, individual's decision variables, except known donation, are unobservable to the others. It must be noted that individuals form beliefs about α_i based on x_{ik}, not x_i. This result is because of the definition of anonymous donation: anonymous donation is unobservable to others, while known donation is observable. It is important that anonymous donors ($x_{ai} \neq 0$ and $x_{ki} = 0$) and non-donors ($x_{ai} = 0$ and $x_{ki} = 0$) are considered the same by others.

Next, I specify the parameter values and distribution of the individual types in this economy. Table 3.1 summarizes the information about the four individual types of my model.

The first type is those with neither altruism nor self-consciousness: $\alpha_i = 0$ and $\beta_i = 0$. I refer to this type as the "selfish". The second type is those with altruism but no self-consciousness: $\alpha_i = \bar{\alpha}$ and $\beta_i = 0$, where $\bar{\alpha} \in (0, 1)$. I refer to this type as "pure altruists". The third type is those with no altruism but with self-consciousness: $\alpha_i = 0$ and $\beta_i = \bar{\beta}$, where $\bar{\beta} \in (0, 1)$. I refer to this type as "hypocrites". The last type is the consumer with both altruism and self-consciousness: $\alpha_i = \bar{\alpha}$ and $\beta_i = \bar{\beta}$. I refer to this type as "impure altruists". Furthermore, I assume that each type has a population of N_s, N_h, N_{pa}, and N_{ia}, respectively. Table 3.1 summarizes the information about these individual types.

Table 3.1 Individual types

Type	α	β	Population
Selfish	0	0	N_s
Pure altruist	$\bar{\alpha}$	0	N_{pa}
Hypocrite	0	$\bar{\beta}$	N_h
Impure altruist	$\bar{\alpha}$	$\bar{\beta}$	N_{ia}

3.3 Main Points of the Model

3.3.1 Who Makes a Giving?

I briefly describe what happens in the model. First, I ask who makes a giving. Pure altruists and impure altruists who are $\alpha > 0$ clearly give, because giving directly yields utility for them. However, it is important that hypocrites (who are not altruistic) also have the possibility to give, though hypocrites are not altruistic ($\alpha = 0$). This is because hypocrites are self-conscious ($\beta > 0$). They possibly give not because they are altruistic but because they want to be seen as altruistic.

3.3.2 Who Makes Anonymous Giving?

One important task is to determine who donates anonymously. The answer is pure altruists. There are two reasons for this. First, because anonymous giving, by definition, cannot be observed by others, anonymous donors and non-donors are considered the same (i.e., the same $\hat{\alpha}_i$). Second, the types who are concerned with their own reputation ($\beta_i \neq 0$) want to be seen as altruistic (i.e., as donors); consequently, they never prefer anonymous to known donation. Then, the pure altruists (who are altruistic but not self-conscious) are the only type who may make anonymous donations. Pure altruists must be indifferent to whether a giving is known or anonymous. I assume that a fraction $A \in (0, 1)$ of pure altruists choose anonymous over known donation, and thus $1 - A$ of them choose known over anonymous donation. I also assume that A can be exogenously controlled by fundraisers by providing check boxes on their Web sites or not. In the next section, I examine the effect of controlling A on the Nash equilibrium.

3.3.3 What Is the Problem?

As mentioned above, there is possibility for hypocrites (who are not altruistic) to give and for pure altruists to give anonymously. The problem lies in the effect of the existence of anonymous giving that can impair the incentive of hypocrites to give. Suppose that a substantial number of pure altruists switch from known to anonymous giving. First, known donors are no longer reputable compared with anonymous donors. Second, the reputation of non-donors, in contrast, is enhanced because people think that some perceived non-donors are actually altruistic anonymous donors. These two effects reduce the incentive for potential donors (who are hypocrites) to become donors. In the next section, I examine the equilibrium of the model to show these effects.

3.4 Separating Equilibrium

Hypocrites and impure altruists behave strategically. If both types donate different amounts at the equilibrium, I say that it is a separating equilibrium. Then, there can be two types of separating equilibria: (1) hypocrites mimic pure altruists and (2) hypocrites mimic the selfish. I show that which type of separating equilibrium exists depends on the level of A.

3.4.1 Hypocrites Mimic Pure Altruists

The first type of separating equilibria is that hypocrites mimic pure altruists.[2] In the following, I show beliefs and conditions under which this type of separating equilibrium exists.

Beliefs
The on- and off-path beliefs are as follows:

- If $x_{ki} = 0$, it is a hypocrite with probability 0, pure altruist with probability $\frac{AN_{pa}}{N_s+AN_{pa}}$, and selfish with probability $\frac{N_s}{N_s+AN_{pa}}$.
- If $0 < x_{ki} < \bar{\alpha}y_i$, it is a hypocrite with probability 1.
- If $x_{ki} = \bar{\alpha}y_i$, it is a hypocrite with probability $\frac{N_h}{N_h+(1-A)N_{pa}}$ and pure altruist with probability $\frac{(1-A)N_{pa}}{N_h+(1-A)N_{pa}}$.
- If $\bar{\alpha}y_i < x_{ki} < \bar{\alpha}y_i + \phi_i$, it is a hypocrite with probability 1.
- If $\bar{\alpha}y_i + \phi_i \leq x_{ki}$, it is an impure altruist with probability 1.

ϕ_i is defined later.

Selfish
People without self-consciousness, by definition, simply solve their classical optimization problems with respect to donation and private goods, but not their images. In short, it is the simple warm-glow setup I see above. It is obvious that the selfish spend all of their income on private goods. For the selfish, $c_i = y_i$ and $x_i = 0$.

Pure Altruist
Pure altruists also face their classical optimization problems without image motivation. The solution to this problem is $c_i = (1 - \bar{\alpha})y_i$ and $x_i = \bar{\alpha}y_i$. Because $\hat{\alpha}_i$ does not appear in their optimization problems, pure altruists are indifferent to the choice between x_a and x_k; both options yield the same utility. Here, I assume that a fraction $A \in (0, 1)$ of the pure altruists choose anonymous over known donation, and thus $1 - A$ of them choose known over anonymous donation. As a result, the introduction of the option of anonymous giving makes some pure altruists switch from known

[2]For simplicity, I consider the case in which all hypocrites behave as a group. This does not change the result much as long as I focus on the symmetric equilibrium.

to anonymous giving. I should not overlook that the total donation amount of pure altruists is independent of A.

Hypocrite and Impure Altruist

It is most important to examine the conditions under which even hypocrites make donations in spite of their selfish nature. By making donations, they mimic pure altruists (a good type) to enhance their reputations.

First, consider the behavior of a hypocrite. Note that there are three options for hypocrites to choose, $x_{ki} = 0$, $x_{ki} = \bar{\alpha} y_i$, or $x_{ki} = \bar{\alpha} y_i + \phi_i$. If they choose $x_{ki} = 0$, they are in the same group as selfish. If they choose $x_{ki} = \bar{\alpha} y_i$, they are in the same group as pure altruists. If they choose $\bar{\alpha} y_i + \phi_i$, they are in the same group as impure altruists. Comparing the three options above, I can derive the conditions for hypocrites to choose $x_{ki} = \bar{\alpha} y_i$ over $x_{ki} = 0$ and $x_{ki} = \bar{\alpha} y_i + \phi_i$:

$$ln\,(y_i - \bar{\alpha} y_i - \phi_i) + \bar{\beta} I(\bar{\alpha}) \leq ln(y_i - \bar{\alpha} y_i) + \bar{\beta} I\left(\frac{(1-A)N_{pa}}{N_h + (1-A)N_{pa}}\bar{\alpha}\right), \tag{3.5}$$

$$ln(y_i) + \bar{\beta} I\left(\frac{AN_{pa}}{N_s + AN_{pa}}\bar{\alpha}\right) \leq ln(y_i - \bar{\alpha} y_i) + \bar{\beta} I\left(\frac{(1-A)N_{pa}}{N_h + (1-A)N_{pa}}\bar{\alpha}\right). \tag{3.6}$$

Here, ϕ_i is defined as the value that satisfies (3.5) with equality; hence, (3.5) is satisfied. In short, if (3.6) is satisfied, hypocrites mimic pure altruists. Next, consider the behavior of the impure altruist. It can be easily checked that if (3.5) is satisfied, the impure altruist prefers $x_{ki} = \bar{\alpha} y_i + \phi_i$ to $x_{ki} = \bar{\alpha} y_i$.

In summary, if (3.6) is satisfied, the above beliefs and hypocrite: $x_{ki} = \bar{\beta} y_i$, impure altruist: $x_{ki} = \bar{\beta} y_i + \phi_i$ are the separating equilibrium. Therefore, the question of "when does this separating equilibrium exist" is equivalent to the question "when is the condition (3.6) satisfied". I can derive the following proposition.

Proposition (Hypocrites mimic Pure Altruists) *If A is sufficiently small, there exists a separating equilibrium in which hypocrites mimic pure altruists.*

Proof The left hand side represents the utility when they join the group of non-donors ($x_{ki} = 0$), while the right hand side represents the utility when hypocrites join the group of known donors ($x_{ki} = \bar{\alpha} y_i$). The second term on the left hand side of (3.6) is increasing in A,

$$\frac{\partial \bar{\beta} \ln I\left(\frac{AN_{pa}}{N_s + AN_{pa}}\bar{\alpha}\right)}{\partial A} > 0, \tag{3.7}$$

and the right hand side of (3.6) is decreasing in A,

$$\frac{\partial \bar{\beta} \ln I\left(\frac{(1-A)N_{pa}}{N_h + (1-A)N_{pa}}\bar{\alpha}\right)}{\partial A} < 0. \tag{3.8}$$

Therefore, if A takes a sufficiently large value, (3.6) is difficult to satisfy. In other words, if A takes a sufficiently small value, (3.6) is satisfied, and this separating equilibrium exists. □

The interpretation of these two inequalities is the core of this study. I refer to (3.8) as the "decrease effect", and (3.7) as the "blend effect". I first note that pure altruists are thought to be of a "good" type compared with the selfish and hypocrites because pure altruists have higher altruism. Next, the group reputation is formed according to the ratio of "good" (altruistic) group members. To interpret (3.8), suppose that some of the pure altruists (a "good" type) switch from known $((x_{ai}, x_{ki}) = (0, \bar{\alpha} y_i))$ to anonymous donation $((x_{ai}, x_{ki}) = (\bar{\alpha} y_i, 0))$. Such a switch implies a decrease in the "good" type in the group of known donors $(x_{ki} = \bar{\alpha} y_i)$. Then, to hypocrites, joining the group of known donors $(x_{ki} = \bar{\alpha} y_i)$ becomes less attractive. This decrease effect corresponds to inequality (3.8). The first inequality (3.7) represents the blend effect. Because anonymous donation is unobservable, people now think that some perceived non-donors are actually anonymous donors. Some fraction of non-donors are of the good type $(\hat{\alpha} = \frac{AN_{pa}}{N_s + AN_{pa}} \bar{\alpha} > 0)$. As a result, the existence of anonymous donors enhances the reputation of non-donors, and joining the group of non-donors $(x_{ki} = 0)$ becomes more attractive to hypocrites. Here, anonymous donors blend into non-donors. This blend effect corresponds to inequality (3.7).

Finally, I should check the existence of other equilibria if this separating equilibrium exists. By intuitive criterion, off-path belief is necessarily "impure altruist with possibility of 1 if $x_{ki} > \bar{\alpha} y_i + \phi_i$." Under this belief, pooling equilibrium does not exist if the impure altruist at the pooling equilibrium does not gain more than $x_{ki} = \bar{\alpha} y_i + \phi_i$; equivalently, if

$$
\begin{aligned}
(1-\bar{\alpha}) ln(y_i - \bar{\alpha} y_i) + \bar{\alpha} ln(\bar{\alpha} y_i) + \bar{\beta} I\left(\frac{(1-A)N_{pa} + N_{ia}}{N_h + (1-A)N_{pa} + N_{ia}} \bar{\alpha}\right) \\
< (1-\bar{\alpha}) ln(y_i - \bar{\alpha} y_i - \phi_i) + \bar{\alpha} ln(\bar{\alpha} y_i + \phi_i) + \bar{\beta} I(\bar{\alpha}), \qquad (3.9)
\end{aligned}
$$

pooling equilibrium does not exist. This study assumes (3.9) and focuses only on separating equilibria.

To sum up, the larger A is, the more difficult it is for this separating equilibrium to exist.

3.4.2 *Hypocrites Mimic the Selfish*

The second type of separating equilibrium is that hypocrites mimic the selfish. In the following, I show beliefs and conditions under which this type of separating equilibrium exists.

Beliefs
The on- and off-path beliefs are as follows:

- If $x_{ki} = 0$, it is a hypocrite with probability $\frac{N_h}{N_s+AN_{pa}+N_h}$, pure altruist with probability $\frac{AN_{pa}}{N_s+AN_{pa}+N_h}$, and selfish with probability $\frac{N_s}{N_s+AN_{pa}+N_h}$.
- If $0 < x_{ki} < \bar{\beta} y_i$, it is a hypocrite with probability 1.
- If $x_{ki} = \bar{\beta} y_i$, it is a pure altruist with probability 1.
- If $\bar{\beta} y_i < x_{ki} < \bar{\alpha} y_i + \delta_i$, it is a hypocrite with probability 1.
- If $\bar{\alpha} y_i + \delta_i \leq x_{ki}$, it is an impure altruist with probability 1.

δ_i is defined later.

Selfish and Pure Altruist
The behavior of the selfish and pure altruist is the same as before. They simply solve their classical optimization problems with respect to donation and private goods, but not their images. For the selfish, $c_i = y_i$ and $x_i = 0$. For the pure altruist, the solution is $c_i = (1 - \bar{\alpha})y_i$ and $x_i = \bar{\alpha} y_i$. A fraction A of pure altruists choose anonymous over known donation, and thus $1 - A$ of them choose known over anonymous donation.

Hypocrite and Impure Altruist
First, consider the behavior of the hypocrite. Note that there are three options for hypocrites to choose, $x_{ki} = 0$, $x_{ki} = \bar{\alpha} y_i$, or $x_{ki} = \bar{\alpha} y_i + \delta_i$. If they choose $x_{ki} = 0$, they are in the same group as selfish. If they choose $x_{ki} = \bar{\alpha} y_i$, they are in the same group as pure altruists. If they choose $\bar{\alpha} y_i + \delta_i$, they are in the same group as impure altruists. Comparing the three options above, I can derive the conditions for hypocrites to choose $x_{ki} = 0$ over $x_{ki} = \bar{\alpha} y_i$ and $x_{ki} = \bar{\alpha} y_i + \delta_i$:

$$ln(y_i - \bar{\alpha} y_i - \delta_i) + \bar{\beta} I(\bar{\alpha}) \leq ln(y_i) + \bar{\beta} I(\frac{AN_{pa}}{N_s + N_h + AN_{pa}} \bar{\alpha}), \tag{3.10}$$

$$ln(y_i - \bar{\alpha} y_i) + \bar{\beta} I(\bar{\alpha}) \leq ln(y_i) + \bar{\beta} I\left(\frac{AN_{pa}}{N_s + N_h + AN_{pa}} \bar{\alpha}\right). \tag{3.11}$$

Here, δ_i is defined as the value that satisfies (3.10) with equality; hence, (3.10) is satisfied. In short, if (3.11) is satisfied, hypocrites mimic the selfish. Next, consider the behavior of the impure altruist. It can be easily checked that if (3.10) is satisfied, the impure altruist prefers $x_{ki} = \bar{\alpha} y_i + \delta_i$ to $x_{ki} = \bar{\alpha} y_i$.

In summary, if (3.11) is satisfied, the above beliefs and hypocrite: $x_{ki} = 0$, impure altruist: $x_{ki} = \bar{\beta} y_i + \delta_i$ are the separating equilibrium. Therefore, the question of "when does this separating equilibrium exist" is equivalent to the question "when is the condition (3.11) satisfied." I can derive the following proposition.

Proposition (Hypocrites Mimic the Selfish) *If A is sufficiently large, there exists a separating equilibrium in which hypocrites mimic the selfish.*

Proof The left hand side represents the utility when hypocrites join the group of known donors ($x_{ki} = \bar{\alpha} y_i$), while the right hand side represents the utility when they join the group of non-donors ($x_{ki} = 0$). The second term on the right hand side of (3.6) is increasing in A,

$$\frac{\partial I\left(\frac{AN_{pa}}{N_s+N_h+AN_{pa}}\bar{\alpha}\right)}{\partial A} > 0. \tag{3.12}$$

Therefore, if A takes a sufficiently large value, (3.11) is satisfied, and this separating equilibrium exists. □

Equation (3.12) represents the blend effect. Because anonymous donation is unobservable, people now think that some perceived non-donors are actually anonymous donors. Some fraction of non-donors is of the "good" type ($\hat{\alpha} = \frac{AN_{pa}}{N_s+N_h+AN_{pa}}\bar{\alpha} > 0$). As a result, the existence of anonymous donors enhances the reputation of non-donors, and joining the group of non-donors ($x_{ki} = 0$) becomes more attractive to hypocrites. Here, anonymous donors blend into non-donors.

Finally, I should check the existence of other equilibria if this separating equilibrium exists. By intuitive criterion, off-path belief is necessarily "impure altruist with possibility of 1 if $x_{ki} > \bar{\alpha}y_i + \phi_i$." Under this belief, pooling equilibrium does not exist if the impure altruist at the pooling equilibrium does not gain more than $x_{ki} = \bar{\alpha}y_i + \phi_i$; equivalently, if

$$\begin{aligned}(1-\bar{\alpha})ln(y_i - \bar{\alpha}y_i) + \bar{\alpha}ln(\bar{\alpha}y_i) + \bar{\beta}I(\frac{(1-A)N_{pa} + N_{ia}}{N_h + (1-A)N_{pa} + N_{ia}}\bar{\alpha}) \\ < (1-\bar{\alpha})ln(y_i - \bar{\alpha}y_i - \phi_i) + \bar{\alpha}ln(\bar{\alpha}y_i + \phi_i) + \bar{\beta}I(\bar{\alpha}),\end{aligned} \tag{3.13}$$

pooling equilibrium does not exist. This study assumes (3.13) and focuses only on separating equilibria.

To sum up, the larger A is, the easier it is for this separating equilibrium to exist.

3.4.3 Summary of the Results

The main results obtained above are as follows: if A is large, a separating equilibrium "hypocrites mimic the selfish" exists. Conversely, if A is small, a separating equilibrium "hypocrites mimic pure altruists" exists.

In more detail, while impure altruists are averse to mimicry by hypocrites, pure altruists do not care about it. Thus, hypocrites mimic the "target" pure altruists. Then, existence of anonymous donors indicates (1) decrease in the best target for hypocrites to mimic and (2) increase in the good type in the non-donor group. Therefore, if there are many anonymous donors, hypocrites do not give.

This is because fundraisers have to care about the level of A. To raise funds from hypocrites and maximize the total amount of donation, fundraisers should make A lower.

3.5 Policy Implication and Discussions

The donation amount varies according to an exogenously determined A. This result raises a question: can fundraisers control A and expected A? In this section, I discuss one practical method to control both A and expected A.

Currently, many fundraisers solicit contributions via the Internet in addition to normal fundraising activities. On their Web sites, some fundraisers including Anna Marie's Alliance, the Minnesota AIDS Project, and the Network for Good place check boxes for donors to select either anonymous or known donations. Figure 3.1 shows how such a typical Web site looks. The list in Table 3.2 shows which fundraisers place check boxes and which do not on their Web sites. Donors fill out not only information about the donation amount, name, address, and credit card number but also the check box, "*I prefer to make this donation anonymously.*" However, some organizations, such as the American Cancer Society, the American Red Cross, and Doctors Without Borders do not provide such check boxes on their Web sites. Without a special request, only known donation is available for donors. I see that more than a few fundraisers explicitly offer opportunities for anonymous giving. By providing the check boxes, these fundraisers intend to make it convenient to donate anonymously. The problem, however, is that when facing the choice, donors assume that fundraisers have provided the check box as a response to many requests from a substantial number of anonymous donors. In other words, the check box exaggerates the number of anonymous donors. Here, A is expected to be higher than that it actually is.

To keep both A and expected A lower, fundraisers can remove this type of check box. Instead, they can implement some type of small foot cost on anonymous giving and accept anonymous donations only as an exception. For instance, to give anonymously, donors have to send an e-mail to fundraisers in addition to filling out the personal information form. Then, those who require anonymity choose anonymous giving with a small effort, while those who are indifferent to whether the donation is anonymous choose known giving. An important experimental finding is reported in Andreoni and Petrie (2004). They show that if examinees give subjects an option to donate anonymously, subjects increase their giving. Note that the subjects mainly

Table 3.2 Fundraisers with check boxes

With check boxes	Without check boxes
Minnesota AIDS project	American cancer society
Anna Marie's alliance	American red cross
Akahane Kyodo Bokin	Big brothers big sisters of America
Ronald McDonalds' house charities	Sierra club
	Doctors without borders
	Feed the children
	Oxfam America
	United Nations Children's fund

increase known giving, not anonymous giving. Their finding is not inconsistent with my theoretical results, because it corresponds to the case of low A in my model. My model predicts that if A is small, impure altruists increase known giving above their ideal amount. This is what Andreoni and Petrie (2004) observe. I also predict that if I make A and expected A sufficiently large, then the subjects would decrease their known giving. Fundraisers should keep the actual A and expected A at a low level and consequently maximize the total donation amount.

References

Andreoni, J. (1989). Giving with impure altruism: Applications to charity and Ricardian equivalence. *Journal of Political Economy*, *97*(6), 1447–1458.

Andreoni, J. (1990). Impure altruism and donations to public goods: A theory of warm-glow giving. *The Economic Journal*, *100*(401), 464–477.

Andreoni, J., & Petrie, R. (2004). Public goods experiments without confidentiality: A glimpse into fund-raising. *Journal of Public Economics*, *88*(7–8), 1605–1623.

Ariely, D., Bracha, A., & Meier, S. (2009). Doing good or doing well? Image motivation and monetary incentives in behaving prosocially. *The American Economic Review*, *99*(1), 544–555.

Benabou, R., & Tirole, J. (2006). Incentives and prosocial behavior. *The American Economic Review*, *96*(5), 1652–1678.

Carpenter, J., & Myers, C. K. (2010). Why volunteer? Evidence on the role of altruism, image, and incentives. *Journal of Public Economics*, *94*(11–12), 911–920.

Crumpler, H., & Grossman, P. J. (2008). An experimental test of warm glow giving. *Journal of Public Economics*, *92*(5–6), 1011–1021.

Palfrey, T. R., & Prisbrey, J. E. (1997). Anomalous behavior in public goods experiments: How much and why? *The American Economic Review*, *87*(5), 829–846.

Rege, M., & Telle, K. (2004). The impact of social approval and framing on cooperation on public good situations. *Journal of Public Economics*, *88*(7–8), 1625–1644.

Soetevent, A. R. (2005). Anonymity in giving in a natural context-a field experiment in 30 churches. *Journal of Public Economics*, *89*(11–12), 2301–2323.

Tamura, M. (2012). (2012) Anonymous giving as a vice: An application of image motivation. *Theoretical Economics Letters*, *2*(4), 385–390.

Chapter 4
A Signaling Explanation for Political Parties and Advertisements

Abstract Many politicians, in an election, join political parties and create political advertisements. Political advertisements take many forms including TV commercial, Web sites, and posters, which are often criticized for wasting money. This study sheds lights on their positive aspect: they function as signals to voters under asymmetric information. In the election, candidates' policy preferences (e.g., preferences for income redistribution) are uncertain for voters. Candidates use political parties and advertisements to signal their hidden preference to the voters. Investigating a multi-period version of Snyder and Ting (2002) with the possibility of reelection, I show that political parties are not sufficient signals to reveal politicians' types. Political advertisements work as a complementary signal to political parties. With political parties and advertisements, voters can elect their favorable candidates adequately. Even if the advertisements are a waste of money, they contribute to voting for favored candidates.

Keywords Political party · Political advertisements · Signaling

4.1 Introduction

Politicians often send signals to voters. Notable examples are political parties and political advertisements. Many politicians and candidates join some political parties that issue manifestos. Almost all political candidates make their posters before the election. They sometimes spend enormous amounts of money on media advertising. Such political parties and advertisements are often criticized for wasting money. However, this study sheds lights on their positive aspect: they function as signals to voters under asymmetric information.

Because candidates' types are hidden in the election and unknown to voters, candidates send signals to differentiate themselves from other candidates. Snyder and Ting (2002) show that if politicians' types are uncertain to voters, parties function as brand names (signals) that ensure the quality of the politicians to some extent. Since belonging to a party implies that the candidate's policy is close to the party's ideal policy, it conveys information about the hidden types of the politicians. Then, what

M. Tamura, *Economic Signals*, Development Bank of Japan Research Series, https://doi.org/10.1007/978-981-10-8938-1_4

is the role of political advertisements? Do they work as signals? Is it substitute or compliment to political parties? This chapter is based on Tamura (2018). It extends Snyder and Ting (2002) to the dynamic model with the possibility of reelection and answers these questions. The answer is that political parties are not sufficient signals, and political advertisements work as a compliment to political parties.

One particular characteristic of reelections is that after one term in office, the hidden type of incumbent is completely revealed to the voters. On the other hand, candidates who run for election for the first time can reveal their types only by joining political parties. Then, the fact that the types of candidates are revealed to the voters can be an advantage for some of them; however, this can serve as a disadvantage for other candidates. This is because some incumbents in the party are less favorable to the voters in reality than expected. In my model, there are three types of candidates: (1) a candidate who cannot win at all; (2) a candidate who wins only once and is not reelected; and (3) a candidate who wins, and after one term in office, gets reelected. Then, there is a possibility that political advertisements would be run even if it is simply a waste of money, in the sense of Milgrom and Roberts (1986). Candidates who can be reelected (and hence, ex-post good) have the incentive to differentiate themselves from candidates who can win office only once. With advertisements, voters can elect only the ex-post good candidates.

In Sect. 4.2, I review the main results of Snyder and Ting (2002). In Sect. 4.3, I introduce reelection to the basic model of Snyder and Ting (2002), thereby investigating the model in a dynamic environment: there is another election after one term in office. I find that political parties do not provide sufficient signals in the election. In Sect. 4.4, I examine the incentive of political advertisements. Political advertisements are complementary to political parties. Section 4.5 considers the difference between political parties and advertisements. Section 4.6 summarizes the main results.

4.2 Function of a Political Party

What is the role of a political party? Why do politicians act not as one person but as a group? Snyder and Ting (2002) answers this question. There are three agents: voters, politicians, and political parties. (1) The voters want to elect politicians whose political preferences are close to theirs. However, politicians' preferences are unknown to the voters. This is undesirable even for politicians whose hidden preferences are actually close to the voters'. (2) There are two meanings to politicians' joining the parties. First, the fact that the politician has joined the party is revealed to the voters. Second, if the politician joins the party, he/she has to obey to the party's policy preference. Thus, joining the party provides disutility to politicians whose preferences are far from those of the party. (3) Therefore, party membership informs voters that a politician's hidden preferences are actually close to the party's preferences.

4.3 The Model with Reelection

4.3.1 Timing of the Model

First, adding reelection to the basic model of Snyder and Ting (2002), I would like to show that political parties are not sufficient signals. Snyder and Ting (2002) prove that parties function as brand names that ensure the quality of politicians to some extent. Since belonging to a party implies that the politician's policy is close to the party's ideal policy, it conveys information about the types of politicians. Snyder and Ting (2002), however, consider a static model in which there is one election and one term in office. On the other hand, politicians can get reelected only in a dynamic model in which there are more than two elections. Adding the second election to the basic model, I analyze the consequence of reelections and the role of political parties.

The key feature of a reelection is that politicians completely reveal their types after one term in office. Although joining a party partially reveals the politician's type, conducting the politician's ideal policy in his/her term of office is assumed to reveal the politician's type. This is because in Snyder and Ting (2002) and my model, politicians' types directly indicate their ideal policies; this is a natural assumption.

There are three players in my model: candidates, political parties, and voters. Although there are two parties, there are numerous candidates and voters. The timing of my model is described as follows, but, in short, my model adds a second period (second election) to the model of Snyder and Ting (2002).

1. First Period Starts. Party Platform Selection.
2. Candidate Nomination and Selection.
3. First Vote. First Term of Office.
4. *Second Period Starts. Candidate Nomination and Selection.*
5. *Second Vote. Second Term of Office.*

1. In the first period, political parties choose their platforms within the policy space $[-1, 1]$, which is observed by all players. Each potential candidate and voter has a preferred policy that lies within $[-1, 1]$ with a uniform distribution. Candidates' preferred policies are unobserved by the voters. Potential candidates choose to belong to parties or to be unaffiliated.
2. For each party, nature randomly selects one candidate who chooses to belong to that party for the election. This process means that parties cannot observe the candidates' hidden types.
3. During the first vote, although voters also cannot observe the candidates' hidden types, they can observe whether or not the candidates belong to the parties. The winner of the election is determined by the plurality rule. The winner of the election holds the office and gains a payoff. After one term in office, a politician's type is completely revealed to both parties and voters.

4. In the next period, the incumbent decides whether to run for reelection. The party also decides whether the incumbent will run for reelection or not. If the incumbent does not run for reelection, nature again selects a new candidate for that party. In addition, nature randomly selects one candidate who chooses to belong to the other party for the election.
5. In the second election, the winner is decided by plurality rule. The winner of the second election also holds the office and gains the same payoff as in the first election.

I should note that the decision to run for reelection is made by both the politician and the party to which he or she belongs. First, running for reelection must be profitable to the politician who now holds office. Second, the party must nominate a candidate for reelection who is more likely to win office than a newly nominated politician is. In other words, a politician runs for reelection only if the probability of his reelection is higher than that of a new candidate whose ideal policy is unknown to the public.

The remaining functional setup is as follows. The policy space is between $[-1, 1]$. The payoff of politician i with an ideal point z_i who is affiliated with party k and wins office is

$$w - c - \alpha(x_k - z_i)^2, \tag{4.1}$$

where w denotes the rent of taking office, $c \in [0, w)$ denotes the cost of taking office, x_k denotes the policy of political party k, and coefficient $\alpha > 0$. On the other hand, if they do not win, their payoff is 0. Voters lie in $[-1, 1]$ with uniform distribution. Voters lie in $[-1, 1]$ with uniform distribution. The expected payoff of the median voter (who is located at 0) if party k's candidate i wins is

$$E\big[-(0 - z_i)^2\big] = -(0 - \mu_i)^2 - \sigma_i^2, \tag{4.2}$$

where μ_i denotes the mean, and σ_i denotes the variance of the candidate in party i.

4.3.2 The Equilibrium

I deal with the case in which there are two political parties and both choose platform $x_i = 0$.[1] This is natural because the median voter is also at 0. In words, both parties target the median voter, and they suggest the same policy.

First, consider the second period. The incumbent who won the first period election has to compete against a candidate of the other party. I call this new candidate of the

[1] This is the equilibrium when $\theta < \sqrt{3}/2$ in Snyder and Ting (2002).

opponent party "challenger". Then, the expected payoff of the median voter at 0 for the challenger is

$$-(0-0)^2 - \frac{\theta^2}{3}, \tag{4.3}$$

where $\theta \equiv \sqrt{\frac{w-c}{\alpha}}$. Note that candidates join a political party if their expected payoff is larger than 0, which is the payoff when they do not run for election. In short, $w - \alpha(0 - z_i)^2 - c > 0$, and hence, $z_i \in [-\theta, \theta]$. μ_i and σ_i for $z_i \in [-\theta, \theta]$ is 0 and $\frac{1}{3}\theta^2$, respectively. On the other hand, the expected payoff of the median voter at 0 for the incumbent is

$$-(0-z_i)^2 - 0. \tag{4.4}$$

This is because, at the second period, for the hidden type of incumbent to win,

$$-\frac{\theta^2}{3} < -z_i^2. \tag{4.5}$$

In short, if $z_i \in \left[-\frac{\sqrt{3}}{3}\theta, \frac{\sqrt{3}}{3}\theta\right]$, the challenger loses and the incumbent wins. Otherwise, since the challenger is going to win, the incumbent does not run for reelection.

Next, go back to the first election. Note that, in the first election, candidates who join the party (and win) lie in

$$z_i \in \big[-\theta, \theta\big]. \tag{4.6}$$

This is the same result as Snyder and Ting (2002). The candidate's nomination and platform selection are independent of introducing the second election. To sum up, in the first election, candidates $z_i \in \big[-\theta, \theta\big]$ join the party. In the second election, candidates $z_i \in \left[-\frac{\sqrt{3}}{3}\theta, \frac{\sqrt{3}}{3}\theta\right]$ run for reelection. In words, incumbents in the narrower range can only run for reelection and win office.

Based on these politicians' behavior, there are three types of candidates:

Loser: If $z_i \in [-1, -\theta]$ or $z_i \in [\theta, 1]$, he/she does not join a party. I refer to him/her as "loser".

One-time Winner: If $z_i \in [-\theta, -\frac{\sqrt{3}}{3}\theta]$ or $z_i \in [\frac{\sqrt{3}}{3}\theta, \theta]$, he/she joins a party, but does not get reelected. I refer to him/her as "one-time winner".

Two-time Winner: If $z_i \in [-\frac{\sqrt{3}}{3}\theta, \frac{\sqrt{3}}{3}\theta]$, he/she joins a party, and get reelected. I refer to him/her as "two-time winner".

I find that "loser" does not join a party. Therefore, I can say that joining parties work to signal the politicians' types to some extent. I also find that one-time winner are found unfavorable to the voters after one term in office, even though they were elected in the first election.

Because each party selects one candidate, the first voting has three possibilities[2]:

- **One-time Winner versus One-time Winner**
  Both of them join parties; one gets elected with 50% in the first election and does not get reelected.
- **Two-time Winner versus One-time Winner**
  Both of them join parties; one gets elected with 50% in the first election and only the two-time winner gets reelected.
- **Two-time Winner versus Two-time Winner**
  Both of them join parties; one gets elected with 50% in the first election and gets reelected.

As is shown above, joining a party works as a signal to some extent. However, there is still a problem with voting for the most favored candidate. If promising candidates (two-time winners) compete against non-promising candidates (one-time winners), promising candidates have only a 50% chance of winning. This fact implies that political parties are not sufficient signals.

Then, the main result is as follows: incumbents in a narrower range can run for reelection and win office. However, joining a political party does not differentiate between ex-post good politicians (who can get reelected) and ex-post bad politicians (who cannot get reelected).

4.4 The Model with Reelection and Advertisement

4.4.1 Timing of the Model

As is seen in the previous section, political parties are not sufficient signals. Next, by introducing political advertisements in the above-mentioned model, I would like to answer the question: What is the role of political parties? The main result is that political advertisements work as a complementary signal to political parties. Promising (ex-post good) candidates design political advertisements to differentiate themselves from other (ex-ante good) candidates even if it is simply a waste of money.

The timing of the model is as follows. Stage 3 is added to the model described above; in other words, before the first vote, candidates can design political advertisements.

1. First Period Starts. Parties' Platform Selection.
2. Candidate Nomination and Selection.
3. *Candidates' Political Advertisements*
4. First Voting. First Term of Office.
5. *Second Period Starts. Candidate Nomination and Selection.*
6. *Second Voting. Second Term of Office.*

[2]For simplicity, I omit the loser from the following list.

The important point to note is that advertisements neither affect the payoffs of the voters nor convey any information except their quantity; therefore, political advertisements are simply a waste of money in the same sense as in Milgrom and Roberts (1986).

Promising candidates who can win office twice want to design political advertisements to send more signals to the public before the first election. This is because, as seen in the previous section, in the first election, simply joining a party does not differentiate a two-time winner from a one-time winner, while it differentiates a winner from a loser in the first election. To be more precise, in the two parties case, in the equilibrium, each candidate can win the first election with 50%. However, if the candidate were known to be a two-time winner, he/she would win the election with 100%. Then, the candidate has the incentive to reveal his/her hidden type by designing advertisements.

4.4.2 The Equilibrium

Whether or not candidates make political advertisements depends on the opponent's type and policy. I use the same definition of "loser", "one-time winner", and "two-time winner" as before: a candidate is called a loser if $z \in [-1, -\theta]$ or $z \in [\theta, 1]$, one-time winner if $z \in [-\theta, -\frac{\sqrt{3}}{3}\theta]$ or $z \in [\frac{\sqrt{3}}{3}\theta, \theta]$, and two-time winner if $z \in [-\frac{\sqrt{3}}{3}\theta, \frac{\sqrt{3}}{3}\theta]$. As before, a one-time winner cannot win the reelection and a two-time winner can.

Because each party selects one candidate, the first vote has three possibilities:

- One-time Winner versus One-time Winner
  - if $\theta^2 < 2|z_j|^2 - |z_i|^2$, the promising candidate uses both a party and advertisements.
  - if $\theta^2 > 2|z_j|^2 - |z_i|^2$, the promising candidate uses only a party.
- Two-time Winner versus One-time Winner
  - the promising candidate uses both a party and advertisements.
- Two-time Winner versus Two-time Winner
  - if $\theta^2 < |z_j|^2 - \frac{1}{2}|z_i|^2$, the promising candidate uses both a party and advertisements.
  - if $\theta^2 > |z_j|^2 - \frac{1}{2}|z_i|^2$, the promising candidate uses only a party.

Here, let me briefly describe the equilibrium in words. It should be noted that in the "two-time winner versus one-time winner" case, only two-time winners use both a party and advertisements. In short, with advertisements, the voters can distinguish a two-time winner from a one-time winner, whereas, in the previous section without advertisements, they cannot distinguish the two types. Then, by voting for the candidates who use advertisements, the voters can select a favorable candidate in the election. The implication is also similar in the other situations. If the candidates are located far enough apart, the promising candidate joins a party and also uses advertisements. With advertisements, voters can distinguish promising and favorable candidates in the election. From these results, I can conclude that political advertisements work as a complement to political parties. In the following, I investigate each equilibrium in more detail.

Equilibrium: One-time Winner versus One-time Winner

In the first case, both candidates i and j are one-time winners. I assume that i is closer to the median voter than j. As a result, at the equilibrium, if $\theta^2 < 2|z_j|^2 - |z_i|^2$, then the following is true:

- The loser does not join a party, does not make advertisements, and cannot win at all.
- One-time winner j joins a party, does not make advertisements, and cannot win the first election.
- One-time winner i joins a party, makes advertisements $ad_i = w - c - \alpha {z_j}^2$, and wins the first election with 100%, but does not get reelected.

If $\theta^2 > 2|z_j|^2 - |z_i|^2$, then the following is true:

- The loser does not join a party, does not make advertisements, and cannot win at all.
- One-time winner i and j join parties, do not make advertisements, and can win the first election with 50%, but do not get reelected.

Note that the belief of voters is formed rationally[3] as in Snyder and Ting (2002).

Let us verify that the above is the equilibrium. Suppose that candidate j's strategy is joining a party and making no advertisement. In the following, I check whether or not candidate i's best response is the above strategy. Note that there are three options for the candidates to choose: (1) only join a party, (2) only make advertisements, and (3) both join a party and make advertisements.

For candidate i, option (1) gives the gain as

$$\frac{1}{2}[(w - c - \alpha z_i^2)]. \tag{4.7}$$

This is because both i and j are seen as being in the same group, and candidate i's probability of winning is $\frac{1}{2}$.

[3]To be precise, the belief is as follows: (i) no party joining and $ad < w - c$: then, the candidate is z_j or loser; (ii) no party joining and $ad \geq w - c$: then the candidate is z_i; (iii) party joining and $ad < w - c - \alpha z_j^2$: then, the candidate is z_j; and (iv) party joining and $ad \geq w - c - \alpha z_j^2$: then, the candidate is z_i.

Next, in option (2), candidate i only makes advertisements. What amount of advertisements does candidate i pay for? The answer is

$$ad_i = w - c. \tag{4.8}$$

Candidate i has to pay $w - c$ as advertisements because he/she has to differentiate from candidate j and the non-party-affiliated candidate. If a candidate would win, he/she would gain $w - c$ in the first term of office. Therefore, candidate i pays the larger amount $w - c$ to differentiate him/herself from the other candidates and win the election. Then, for candidate i, option (2) gives the gain as

$$w - c - ad_i = (w - c) - (w - c) \tag{4.9}$$

$$= 0. \tag{4.10}$$

In option (3), candidate i joins a party and additionally makes advertisements. Though joining a party works for candidate i to differentiate him/herself from the unaffiliated candidate, advertisements work to differentiate him/herself from the other party-affiliated candidate. Therefore, the amount of advertisements is

$$ad_i = w - c - \alpha z_j^2, \tag{4.11}$$

which is equal to the gain of candidate j, since j cannot pay that amount of money even if the candidate can win the election. Then, the voters can elect the better candidate even in the first election. For candidate i, option (3) gives the gain as

$$(w - c - \alpha z_i^2) - (w - c - \alpha z_j^2) \tag{4.12}$$

$$= \alpha z_j^2 - \alpha z_i^2. \tag{4.13}$$

Comparing options (1), (2), and (3), I can say that candidates' best response depends on their relative positions. If $\theta^2 < 2|z_j|^2 - |z_i|^2$, candidate i chooses option (3) and gets elected. If $\theta^2 > 2|z_j|^2 - |z_i|^2$, candidate i chooses option (1) and gets elected with probability $\frac{1}{2}$. On the other hand, it is clear that in both cases, candidate j's best response is joining a party and making no advertisement. Therefore, I can conclude that these strategies of i and j are the equilibrium.

Equilibrium: Two-time Winner versus One-time Winner

In the next case, one candidate i is a two-time winner and the other candidate j is a one-time winner. I assume that i is closer to the median voter than j. At the equilibrium, the following is true:

- The loser does not join a party, does not make advertisements, and cannot win at all.

- One-time winner j joins a party, does not make advertisements, and cannot win the first election.
- Two-time winner i joins a party, makes advertisements $ad_i = w - c - \alpha {z_j}^2$, wins the first election with 100%, and gets reelected.

Note that the belief of voters is formed rationally[4] as in Snyder and Ting (2002).

Let me verify that the above is the equilibrium. Suppose that candidate j's strategy is joining a party and making no advertisement. In the following, I check whether or not candidate i's best response is the above strategy. Note that there are three options for the candidates to choose: (1) only join a party, (2) only make advertisements, and (3) both join a party and make advertisements.

For candidate i, option (1) gives the gain as

$$\frac{1}{2}[(w - c - \alpha z_i^2) + (w - c)]. \tag{4.14}$$

This is because both i and j are seen as being in the same group and candidate i's probability of winning is $\frac{1}{2}$.

Next, in option (2), candidate i only makes advertisements. What amount of advertisements does candidate i pay for? The answer is

$$ad_i = w - c. \tag{4.15}$$

Candidate i has to pay $w - c$ as advertisements because he/she has to differentiate from candidate j and the non-party-affiliated candidate. If a candidate would win, he/she would gain $w - c$ in the first term of office. Therefore, candidate i pays the larger amount $w - c$ to differentiate him/herself from the other candidates and win the election. Then, for candidate i, option (2) gives the gain as

$$2(w - c) - ad_i = 2(w - c) - (w - c) \tag{4.16}$$

$$= w - c. \tag{4.17}$$

In option (3), candidate i joins a party and makes advertisements. Though joining a party works for candidate i to differentiate him/herself from the unaffiliated candidate, advertisements work to differentiate him/herself from the other party-affiliated candidate. Therefore, the amount of advertisements is

$$ad_i = w - c - \alpha z_j^2, \tag{4.18}$$

which is equal to the gain of the other affiliated candidate, since j cannot pay that amount of money even if he/she can win the election. Voters can then distinguish

[4]To be precise, the belief is as follows: (i) no party joining and $ad < w - c$: then, the candidate is z_j or loser; (ii) no party joining and $ad \geq w - c$: then, the candidate is z_i: (iii) party joining and $ad < w - c - \alpha z_j^2$: then, the candidate is z_j; and (iv) party joining and $ad \geq w - c - \alpha z_j^2$: then, the candidate is z_i.

between the better and worse candidate even in the first election by observing whether the candidates have advertised or not. For candidate i, option (3) gives

$$(w - c - \alpha z_i^2) - (w - c - \alpha z_j^2) + (w - c) \tag{4.19}$$
$$= w - c + \alpha z_j^2 - \alpha z_i^2. \tag{4.20}$$

Comparing options (1), (2), and (3), I can say that candidate i's best strategy is (3) both join a party and make advertisements. As a result, candidate i gets elected. On the other hand, it is clear that candidate j's best response is joining a party and making no advertisement. Therefore, I can conclude that these strategies of i and j are the equilibrium.

Equilibrium: Two-time Winner versus Two-time Winner

In the last case, both candidates i and j are two-time winners. I assume that i is closer to the median voter than j. As a result, at the equilibrium, if $\theta^2 < |z_j|^2 - \frac{1}{2}|z_i|^2$, then the following is true:

- The loser does not join a party, does not make advertisements, and cannot win at all.
- Two-time winner j joins a party, does not make advertisements, and cannot win the first election.
- Two-time winner' i joins a party, makes advertisements $ad_i = 2(w - c) - \alpha {z_j}^2$, wins the first election with 100%, and gets reelected.

  If $\theta^2 > |z_j|^2 - \frac{1}{2}|z_i|^2$, then the following is true:

- The loser does not join a party, does not make advertisements, and cannot win at all.
- One-time winner i and j join parties, do not make advertisements, can win the first election with 50%, and get reelected.

Note that the belief of voters is formed rationally[5] as in Snyder and Ting (2002).

Let me verify that the above is the equilibrium. Suppose that candidate j's strategy is joining a party and making no advertisement. In the following, I check whether or not candidate i's best response is the above strategy. Note that there are three options for the candidates to choose: (1) only join a party, (2) only make advertisements, and (3) both join a party and make advertisements.

For candidate i, option (1) gives the gain as

$$\frac{1}{2}[(w - c - \alpha z_i^2) + (w - c)]. \tag{4.21}$$

[5] To be precise, the belief is as follows: (i) no party joining and $ad < 2(w - c)$: then, the candidate is z_j or loser; (ii) no party joining and $ad \geq 2(w - c)$: then, the candidate is z_i; (iii) party joining and $ad < 2(w - c) - \alpha z_j^2$; then, the candidate is z_j; and (iv) party joining and $ad \geq 2(w - c) - \alpha z_j^2$: then, the candidate is z_i.

This is because both i and j are seen as being in the same group, and the probability of winning is $\frac{1}{2}$.

Next, in option (2), candidate i only makes advertisements. What amount of advertisements does candidate i pay for ? The answer is

$$ad_i = 2(w - c). \tag{4.22}$$

Candidate i has to pay $w - c$ as advertisements because he/she has to differentiate from the candidate j and non-party-affiliated candidate. If candidate j would win, he/she would gain $2(w - c)$ and non-party-affiliated candidate would gain $w - c$ in the first term of office. Therefore, candidate i pays the larger amount $2(w - c)$ to differentiate him/herself from the other candidates and win the election. Then, for candidate i, option (2) gives the gain as

$$2(w - c) - ad_i = 2(w - c) - 2(w - c) \tag{4.23}$$
$$= 0. \tag{4.24}$$

In option (3), candidate i joins a party and makes advertisements. Though joining a party works for the candidate to differentiate him/herself from the unaffiliated candidate, advertisements work to differentiate him/herself from the other party-affiliated candidate. Therefore, the amount of advertisements is

$$ad_i = (w - c - \alpha z_j^2) + (w - c), \tag{4.25}$$

which is equal to the gain of the other affiliated candidate, since j cannot pay that amount of money even if he/she can win the election. The voters can then distinguish between the better and worse candidate even in the first election by observing whether the candidates have advertised or not. For candidate i, option (3) gives

$$\{(w - c - \alpha z_i^2) - [(w - c - \alpha z_j^2) + (w - c)]\} + w - c \tag{4.26}$$
$$= \alpha z_j^2 - \alpha z_i^2. \tag{4.27}$$

Comparing options (1), (2), and (3), I can say that candidates' best response depends on their relative positions. If $\theta^2 < |z_j|^2 - \frac{1}{2}|z_i|^2$, candidate i chooses the option (3) and gets elected. If $\theta^2 > |z_j|^2 - \frac{1}{2}|z_i|^2$, candidate i chooses option (1) and gets elected with probability $\frac{1}{2}$. On the other hand, it is clear that in both cases, candidate j's best response is also joining a party and making no advertisement. Therefore, I can conclude that these strategies by i and j's strategy are the equilibrium.

4.5 Difference Between Political Parties and Political Advertisements

I have found that both political parties and political advertisements work as signals to voters. In this section, I would like to explain in words the difference between political parties and political advertisements.

Basically, political parties work more as efficient signals than advertisements. This is because joining parties costs candidates heterogeneously, while making advertisements costs candidates homogeneously. First, consider the political parties. Candidates who are located further than the parties' ideal policy pay larger cost to join the parties than candidates who are located nearer to the parties' ideal policy. This is seen in (4.1). Next, consider the political advertisements. When candidates make political advertisements, all candidates pay the same cost to make the same amount of advertisements. In short, joining parties is a better signal for promising candidates than advertisements because it costs less.

Therefore, in all cases, promising candidates who are located nearer to the parties' ideal policy first join political parties. However, joining parties is sometimes not enough to differentiate themselves from the other candidates. They need an additional signal, political advertisements, though it is less efficient for promising candidates. When is the first signal, joining a party, not enough? The answer is mainly when the gain of winning an election is very different among candidates (e.g., two-time winner versus one-time winner). Then, candidates have stronger incentives to differentiate themselves from other candidates. They make less efficient political advertisements in addition to joining political parties.

In short, political advertisements work as a complement signal to political advertisements. With the two signals, the promising candidates can make voters distinguish themselves from other candidates. Voters can choose adequate candidates even in the first election.

4.6 Summary

Let me summarize the main points of this chapter. Investigating a multi-period version of Snyder and Ting (2002), I study the signaling aspect of political parties and political advertisements. Political advertisements work as a complementary signal to political parties: political parties are basically more efficient signals. However, candidates who have strong incentives to win and need more signals make advertisements in addition to joining parties.

I can conclude that both political parties and advertisements help voters to adequately choose their ex-post good politicians in the election. Though political advertisements can be regarded as a social cost in the sense that they do not directly yield any utility or gain, they are a signaling tool that conveys correct information about politicians' types.

References

Milgrom, P., & Roberts, J. (1986). Price and advertising signals of product quality. *Journal of Political Economy*, *94*(4), 796–821.

Snyder, J. M, Jr., & Ting, M. M. (2002). An informational rationale for political parties. *American Journal of Political Science*, *46*(1), 90–110.

Tamura, M. (2018) A Signaling Explanation for Political Parties and Advertisements. *Theoretical Economics Letters*, *8*(3), 241–255.

www.ingramcontent.com/pod-product-compliance
Ingram Content Group UK Ltd.
Pitfield, Milton Keynes, MK11 3LW, UK
UKHW022108180926
475695UK00001B/48

* 9 7 8 9 8 1 1 0 8 9 3 7 4 *